To my daughters, Allegra and Zinnia, who bring
me the greatest joy, this book is dedicated to you.

AFGHANISTAN

TAJIKISTAN

PAKISTAN

Delhi

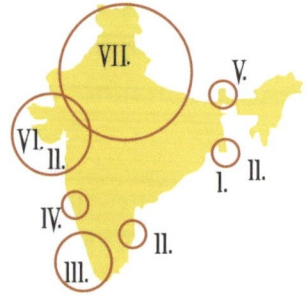

India

NEPAL

Gujarat

BHUTAN

Sikkim

BANGLADESH

MYANMAR

Mumbai
(Bombay)

Upper Deccan
Plateau

Kolkata
(Calcutta)

Goa

VINEGAR

Bay of Bengal

Arabian
Sea

Chennai
(Madras)

Kerala

SRI
LANKA

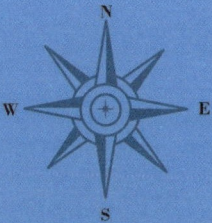

I.   Indo-Chinese (Kolkata)

II. Anglo-Indian (Kolkata, Chennai, Mumbai)

III. Syrian Christian (Kerala)

IV. Goan Portuguese (Goa)

V.   Tibetan Nepalese (Sikkim, Kalimpong, Darjeeling)

VI. Parsi (Gujarat, Mumbai)

VII. Mughal (North India to Upper Deccan)

SEVEN KITCHENS

A JOURNEY THROUGH INDIA'S CULINARY HERITAGE

TORIE TRUE

me:ze
PUBLISHING

Contents

Introduction

Here in Britain, when we think about Indian food, we tend to think of the popular dishes found in curry houses across the nation that were, and still are to some degree, a much-loved cornerstone of our dining scene. Big hitters like vindaloo, biryani and korma are just a few of these familiar favourites – but have you ever taken a step back and wondered where these recipes actually came from and how they evolved into the dishes we know and love today?

Indian cuisine has been shaped by immigration and integration over hundreds of years. Each group of settlers has brought their own influences to this vast land through new ingredients, flavours, techniques and methods which merged with existing traditions to create numerous variations on the originals. The Portuguese, British, Chinese, Tibetan, Nepali, Parsi, Syrian Christian, Mughal and numerous other peoples have all left their imprint on India's food and this has afforded the country's cuisine a remarkable and exciting diversity. Today, the recipes found throughout India weave a complex and nuanced story of its cultural history and heritage.

In my own travels to India over the decades, I have always relished the regional differences across this extraordinary nation. Kerala is so different from Rajasthan and Kolkata is so different from Goa. I have had the opportunity to interact with home cooks, families and professionals who have been generous with their expertise. Their range of culinary traditions fascinated me, setting me on a journey of discovery as I dug deeper into the country's regional cuisines. Alongside visiting India and having the privilege of sampling so many cuisines and learning from locals, I also spent time on historical research at home. The British Library in London holds a remarkable collection of history books, articles and manuscripts and I loved the opportunity to leaf through original recipes from the nineteenth century. Writing this book was part recipe development and part investigative research because I wanted not just to share dishes from India's incredible culinary treasure trove but to provide some historical context for their origins.

I chose to focus on seven key groups and regions of India to give this book its structure. The Portuguese came to Goa in the early fifteenth century and with their arrival, ingredients which are now considered staples of Indian cooking were introduced – tomatoes, chillies and potatoes among others – that gave rise to new dishes combining Portuguese tastes with Indian flair, one of which was the now famous vindaloo.

The British lived in India for over 400 years and devised many recipes to suit their tastes, of which plenty made their way back to Britain and are enjoyed to this day in the UK, India and beyond – kedgeree and mulligatawny are good examples.

Large numbers of Chinese immigrants also settled in India, giving rise to not one but two Chinatowns in Kolkata. Indo-Chinese or Hakka food emerged as a distinctively delicious cuisine that sits between but apart from traditional Indian and Chinese food. Gobi Manchurian remains one of the best things you can do with a cauliflower!

Further back in time, the Mughals arrived from central Asia and brought with them a wealth of new cooking techniques, initially only to the royal courts but later to the broader population. Biryani is a much-loved celebration dish that the Mughals perfected.

The Parsis, also known as Zoroastrians, came to India from Iran – their style of cooking too was unique and dhansak is still a classic dish the world over.

Syrian Christians, one of the oldest Christian communities in the world, can be found in the state of Kerala and their food differs yet again, with other global influences evident in their style of cooking. I love their use of coconut which brings balance and richness to their sauces, not to mention their showstopping duck curry!

Finally, the Nepalis and Tibetans, who settled in the uplands of northeast India, brought techniques that have influenced the dishes of the north. As the climate is cool in the summer and freezing in winter, their food is all about comfort and warmth. On a wet grey day in London, I like nothing more than a bowl of vegetable thukpa and some momos.

As I researched the recipes of all these communities, I adapted them for the modern home kitchen to make each dish accessible and they generally serve four to six people (but if you're cooking for fewer, it's always nice to have leftovers). Each chapter focuses on recipes from a distinct group of people, showcasing some of their most celebrated dishes. Some you may recognise but perhaps hadn't come across their heritage before, and others may well be completely new to you. Like my first cookbook, Seven Kitchens is designed to be easy to follow and invites the reader and home cook on a journey through history as we explore the glorious food and flavours that fall under the umbrella of Indian cuisine.

Author's Notes

How to use this book

This book is split into seven chapters, focusing on recipes from the following groups of people: Goan Portuguese, Anglo-Indian, Indo-Chinese, Parsi, Syrian Christian, Tibetan Nepalese and Mughal. There are vegan, vegetarian, meat and fish dishes, breads, rice and a handful of sweet delights, something to appeal to every palate and persuasion. While the vast majority of ingredients should be familiar to you, there may be some that are entirely new; as we are hugely lucky to be just a click away from sourcing almost anything online in the UK, I have noted where you can find these less common ingredients easily within the recipes and also created a directory of suppliers on page 244.

Ultimately, I want you, the reader of this book, to really enjoy cooking from it, so I have generally avoided recipes that are too tricky, long winded or deep fried (although there are a few of the latter). The popular northeastern Indian snack sel roti, for example, has been left out because the requirements of soaking rice overnight and then blending it for the batter are not going to be top of most people's priorities! I also decided against including a dish called *wachipa* which originated with the Kirat Rai people in Eastern Nepal, tasty as it may be, which uses burnt chicken feathers to create its unique, bitter flavour. I have steered clear of offal too. In short, I would love the recipes in these pages to become part of your own repertoire for go-to meals and family favourites.

On page 242, I've given you some suggestions for recipes to try together and at certain times or occasions. However, please don't feel bound by these or indeed by the chapters I have grouped them into throughout the book. There are no rules here so mix and match, try dishes from different regions in the same sitting, have fun and let your taste buds guide you.

Servings

Most of my recipes serve 4 to 6 people. For my own family of 4, I usually cook a little extra so we can have seconds or keep the leftovers for another day – I also like to have plenty of food ready in case a last-minute guest turns up. I tend to serve a few dishes together, certainly when guests come over, so I may well cook 3 or 4 dishes for a dinner, sometimes more. For 8 guests, I rarely change the proportions of the recipes but may increase the quantity of the main protein by 200-300g, leaving the rest as is. Dal in particular goes a long way and can be quite filling. I typically let guests serve themselves, so they can try everything in the portion size that works for them.

Spice Grinders

THE most useful tool in my kitchen. You will see there are quite a few recipes for making masalas in this book – store-bought spice blends are fine but not quite as good as homemade. They take minutes to rustle up and make a world of difference to the flavour of a finished dish. You can of course use a pestle and mortar, but this takes longer and is harder work! My spice grinder, the James Martin by Wahl model, also has a chopper attachment, which is great at making garlic and ginger pastes or blending tomatoes. Pop one on your wish list; it will save you so much time and energy.

Casserole Pots and Pressure Cookers

For most of the meat curries I cook at home, I use my trusted Le Creuset cast-iron casserole pot, but occasionally I use a pressure cooker to save time (especially useful if you need to make lots of food in a short period, as I did during the photoshoot for this book!).

I grew up with my grandmother using her pressure cooker to make her legendary meat stews and today my mother-in-law often relies on hers to cook her curries. I think pressure cookers are making a bit of a comeback, thanks to safer designs and the ease and speed of cooking with them, not to mention the flavour of the food which is ridiculously good. For those keen to learn more about pressure cooking, I would recommend *Everyday Pressure Cooking* by Catherine Phipps. I have given a brief overview of using a pressure cooker for my recipes below.

The majority of my recipes don't include timings for pressure cooking, because there are several factors involved in calculating this accurately, including the brand and type of pressure cooker you use. Mine is a ProCook Professional stainless steel which I rate highly, but whatever you use, my advice would be to follow the manufacturer's instructions. As a rule of thumb, make sure you brown onions and meat before deglazing (adding liquid). Generally speaking, boneless chicken thighs or chicken breast takes 10 to 15 minutes to cook once the lid goes on, or 20 to 30 minutes for chicken on the bone.

Red meat takes longer: typically between 20 to 30 minutes for thinner, softer cuts while tougher cuts and meat on the bone require at least 30 to 40 minutes. You can check the tenderness of the meat after the initial cooking time by releasing the pressure completely and then removing the lid when it's safe to open, adding liquid and continuing to cook if needed. There is a fine line between cooking meat to perfection and overdoing it, but the more you use your pressure cooker the more comfortable you will be with knowing the timings that work for your model.

Ginger and Garlic

Fresh is always best when using ginger and garlic. To make pastes, I often finely grate the ginger and garlic or put them in my spice grinder with the chopper attachment if I am making a larger quantity. Ginger and garlic paste prepared in this way can easily be frozen in ice cube trays and then used straight from the freezer as needed. That said, for those occasions when we just can't be bothered or are short of time, you can absolutely use store-bought paste.

1

2

3

4

5

6

16

7 8 9

10 11 12

13 14 15

17

18

19

20

21

1. Sichuan peppercorns
2. Fresh curry leaves
3. Dried kudampuli
4. Ajwain/carom seeds
5. Dried Dandicut red chillies
6. Black/brown cardamom
7. Fenugreek seeds
8. Cumin powder
9. Mustard seeds
10. Coriander powder
11. Green cardamom pods
12. Cumin seeds
13. Kashmiri chilli powder
14. Ground turmeric
15. Nigella seeds

16. Cassia bark
17. Cinnamon bark
18. Dried Kashmiri chillies
19. Fresh green chillies
20. Jaggery
21. Dried wood ear mushrooms
22. MSG
23. Asafoetida powder
24. Tamarind block
25. Tamarind pods
26. Tamarind paste
27. Indian bay leaves
28. Black/brown cardamom
29. Dried kokum

22

23

25

26

24

27

28

29

Spice Pantry

Spices are best kept in sealed jars, in a dry place, out of direct sunlight. Always buy the smallest packets so that your spices stay fresh (or team up with someone you can buy larger quantities with and share them out) and aim to use them up within six months.

Essential Spices

Cardamom, Green and Black

Green and black cardamom look and taste very different. Green cardamom is more floral and can be used in both sweet and savoury dishes, while black cardamom has slightly larger pods with a smoky flavour and aroma and is only used whole in savoury dishes. The green cardamom pods can be cooked with or without their husks, though I suggest lightly bashing them open to allow the aromas to come out if using whole. The small seeds inside the green pods can also be ground into a powder but should be used sparingly as the flavour is quite intense.

Cassia and Cinnamon Bark

While they are not the same thing, cinnamon and cassia are related and have similar flavour profiles, so they can be used interchangeably in cooking. Cinnamon is grown across tropical Asia, particularly Sri Lanka, China, Indonesia, Vietnam and Myanmar. The variety native to Sri Lanka is known as 'true cinnamon' while the cassia variety is native to China and is browner in colour, a little hotter in taste and more bark-like in appearance. Sri Lankan cinnamon bark is curled into quills or sticks, and these tend to be best for savoury and sweet baking, whereas cassia is best just for savoury dishes. Ground cinnamon is made from grinding down the cinnamon bark and is more often found in sweet dishes.

Coriander Seeds and Powder

Deliciously light and floral, coriander seeds are found in many Indian curries alongside turmeric and ground cumin. If you buy the seeds whole, dry roast them first to release their fragrant aromas before grinding them to a fine powder.

Cumin Seeds and Powder

Cumin is very distinctive, with a nutty, smoky, warming aroma. When using the seeds whole, add them at the start of a recipe, usually into hot oil. Ground cumin should be added a little later with the vegetable or protein, often alongside ground turmeric and sometimes coriander. Cumin powder looks very similar to coriander powder but their distinct aromas should help you to tell the difference.

Fennel Seeds and Powder

Similar to cumin seeds and ajwain seeds, these have a light green hue and a delicate aniseed flavour. Like other whole spices, they are added at the beginning of the cooking process, usually into hot oil to release their aromas. They can also be made into a powder, which is typically added a little later in the cooking process.

Kashmiri Chilli

You'll see that the chilli powder I talk about in this book is Kashmiri chilli powder. The reason I use this over any other chilli powder is that it adds colour and only mild heat. Regular chilli powder from a supermarket will be a lot hotter, so use it more sparingly. Some people like to use Deggi Mirch, which is a blend of red capsicums and Kashmiri chilli with a more paprika-like flavour, but my go-to is Kashmiri chilli. In some recipes I also mention whole red chillies; you can use whole dried Kashmiri chillies for less heat or whole red chillies of other, hotter, varieties.

Mustard Seeds

I tend to use black or brown mustard seeds that can be used interchangeably but you can also find yellow mustard seeds, which are crushed to make the yellow mustard powder we are all familiar with. The seeds are typically added towards the beginning of a recipe once the oil is hot. They tend to pop and jump out of the pan so you need to add the onion after 10 seconds, which will prevent this happening to the same degree.

Turmeric

This spice is egg-yolk yellow in colour, owing to a pigment known as curcumin, and can be found in most, but not all, Indian savoury dishes. Use ½ to 1 teaspoon for an earthy aroma – any more and the dish can become bitter. Typically, I use the powdered form, although you can use fresh turmeric, for a turmeric chai or latte for example.

Other Spices Used in this Book

Black and White Peppercorns

Peppercorns were historically known as 'black gold' by merchants involved in their lucrative trade. Long before the chilli was introduced by the Portuguese in the fifteenth century, black pepper thrived in India, especially in the southern states. Long pepper, which looks like catkins, was also used to add heat and a delicate sweetness to dishes. Ground white pepper is also used in a few recipes in this book. Both varieties of pepper come from the same plant, but white pepper is a lot hotter and comes from the ripe berries that have had their outer layer removed, whereas black peppercorns are the dried, unripe berries.

Cloves

Use very sparingly so as not to overwhelm a dish. Cloves are generally kept whole and they release the most fragrant aromas. They are used in both sweet and savoury dishes.

Garam Masala

A ground spice blend that is often added towards the end of the cooking process. Garam translates to hot or warm and masala means spice mix. The warming spices often include cinnamon, cloves, cardamom, black pepper, nutmeg, mace and Indian bay leaves. Many households in India have their own version, but you can simply buy yours for ease. In this book there are several masala recipes that are quick to make and easy to store. They all add different aromas to the dishes.

Nigella Seeds

Also known as black onion seeds or *kalonji*, they are the seed from a flowering plant called Nigella Sativa that belongs to the onion family. Small in size but packing a punch, these seeds have a smoky, nutty flavour. They are always kept whole and not ground.

Panch Phoron

Also known as Bengali five spice but not to be confused with Chinese five spice, panch phoron is a spice blend comprising equal quantities of the following whole spices: fenugreek, cumin seeds, fennel seeds, brown or black mustard seeds and nigella seeds. You can easily make your own if you find it hard to source.

Sichuan Peppercorns

These delicious peppercorns from the Sichuan province of China create an irresistible mouth-numbing spiciness with aromatic notes. There are two varieties, red and green, but red are the most commonly used in recipes. Sichuan peppercorns are in fact the dried husks of prickly ash plants, which are part of the citrus family, and unrelated to black, white, pink and green peppercorns. You will find them in some of my recipes in the Indo-Chinese and Tibetan Nepalese chapters. They are easy to source online from Sous Chef and Ottolenghi, as well as in Asian grocery stores.

White Poppy Seeds

I only use white poppy seeds in a few of the recipes in this book. They are harvested from the dried seed pods of the opium poppy, adding texture and a nutty flavour when toasted.

Less Familiar Ingredients

Ajwain Seeds

Also known as carom seeds, bishop's weed or thymol seeds, ajwain is a herb from the Apiaceae family. It has a distinctive wild thyme smell and taste and is often used in pastries and breads. Frying the seeds lightly in oil to begin with releases a nutty flavour.

Asafoetida

Also known as *hing* in Hindi, and more amusingly 'devil's dung stinking gum' due to its sulphurous notes. Don't let this put you off! Asafoetida is bright yellow in colour, even more so than turmeric, and is the gum resin extracted from the ferula plant, a herb in the celery family. I always buy it in powdered form and store it away from direct sunlight. It is sometimes blended with a little wheat or rice flour to stop it caking, so those who want to avoid wheat need to be aware of this – read the small print on the pot you buy! Use it sparingly, never more than quarter of a teaspoon. It is important to add the powder to hot oil or ghee which causes the pungent odour to dissipate and become more oniony and garlicky. In the UK it is relatively easy to find in large supermarkets and certainly in every Asian supermarket. In the US, order it from Burlap & Barrel (see page 247) who mix it with turmeric instead of flour to make it gluten-free.

Curry Leaves

Curry leaves can now be found in some of the larger mainstream supermarkets in the UK. I buy them at my local Indian grocers, many of which sell fresh curry leaves. I always suggest that people buy a few bags to freeze at home and use straight from frozen as needed. They are more flavourful like this compared to dried curry leaves, which don't add much to a dish. When cooking with them, I tend to add a sprig of around 15 leaves to a dish. When they hit oil, they immediately start to infuse your kitchen and will transport you to warm, sunny lands – metaphorically speaking!

Indian Bay Leaves

Also known as *tej patta*, these olive-green leaves have a strong woody aroma and tend to be larger in size than their European counterparts, with three veins running through the length. They have an entirely different flavour profile to European bay, so if you are unable to source them, I suggest leaving them out of the dish altogether. They are commonly found in North Indian dishes, particularly the Mughal recipes in this book.

Jaggery

Also known as *gur*, this unrefined sugar made from sugar cane or palm sap is consumed throughout the Indian subcontinent, Africa, Central America and Brazil. I use it in a few of the recipes, but you can substitute jaggery with light, dark or muscovado brown sugar if you find it hard to source.

Kokum

Kokum is a small red fruit from a plant in the mangosteen family that is grown in India's Western Ghats in the states of Goa, Maharashtra, Karnataka and Kerala. As it ripens, it turns a deep purple. Similar to tamarind, it brings a delicious sourness to dishes. In the UK you can purchase it dried from Asian grocers (I always get mine at Patel Brothers in Tooting) or online.

Kudampuli

This fruit is from the same family as kokum and also known as Malabar tamarind, fish tamarind or brindleberry. It isn't actually tamarind at all but has similar sour qualities. Kudampuli is a fruit from the Garcinia gummi-gutta tree, native to south and southeast Asia, and is commonly used in Keralan cuisine. The ripened green fruit, which looks like a miniature pumpkin, turns black as it dries and has small grooves in its skin.

MSG

There has been much debate and controversy about MSG, or monosodium glutamate, in the past, though generally it is now seen as the harmless flavour enhancer that it is, having been proven to be completely safe. The Burmese food writer MiMi Aye has written many brilliant pieces about MSG and the food podcast Lecker released five episodes on the subject, which I urge you to listen to if you would like to learn more. I have suggested a pinch of MSG in certain recipes in my Tibetan Nepalese and Indo-Chinese chapters. MSG is widely available in supermarkets and shops.

Tamarind

Tamarind has a deliciously sweet and sour flavour whose brown pod-like fruits (see photo on page 11) contain a tangy fibrous pulp. They can be bought whole and broken open when needed, but the pulp is also available in blocks that can be stored in the fridge for months. To use the tamarind in this form, break off a piece and place this in a small bowl, then cover with warm water. Leave it to steep for 10 to 15 minutes and then use your hand to break up the tamarind in the water. Finally, strain it, using the back of a spoon to push the paste through the sieve. Pre-prepared tamarind paste is also available – look out for the medium or light brown jars, which can also be stored in the fridge once opened – and tamarind concentrate is easily found in shops, which you only need to use a little of as its flavour is very strong.

Wood Ear Mushrooms

Also known as black cloud fungus, cloud ear and jelly ear due to their shape, I use these mushrooms in the Tibetan Nepalese recipe for Phingsha on page 164. While they are common in UK woodland, I always buy them dried from Asian grocers or online. To rehydrate the dried mushrooms, soak them in hot water until softened. They expand quite a lot, so you don't need to use too many. They have a pleasingly chewy texture and a mild umami flavour.

Other Pantry Essentials

Fresh Chillies

Similarly to fresh curry leaves, these freeze really well. Look for small green or red chillies that are the size of your little finger; Thai bird's eye chillies will be too hot, and the large green ones will not have enough flavour. I tend to slice them diagonally or lengthways, keeping the membrane and seeds in for extra heat. Remove these if you want less heat as the flesh is milder than the white parts and seeds.

Jarred or Tinned Beans and Pulses

A few recipes request jarred or tinned beans or pulses, such as chickpeas. My preference is always to buy jarred, if I can, for the best flavour. I'd really recommend Bold Bean Co – they are so good you will want to eat them straight from the jar! If you can't find jarred beans or pulses, then of course tinned will also work well.

Oils

For most of the recipes in this book, I have included vegetable, sunflower or rapeseed oil (all neutral oils) in the ingredients list, along with the occasional use of coconut, sesame and olive oil. Any neutral oil will be absolutely fine to use for any of the recipes in the book. If you are frying, I would suggest using vegetable or sunflower oil as they have higher smoke points.

Indo-Chinese

My husband was born in Kolkata, so I've spent quite a bit of time in this bustling metropolis with its faded grandeur and warm smiles. Food is serious business there, and some might say Kolkata offers the best street food in India. Even before one meal is finished, deciding what and where to eat next is always on the agenda. There is one cuisine that Bengalis have a real weakness for and that is the local Indo-Chinese food, sometimes called Tangra, Kolkata Chinese, desi Chinese or simply Hakka, on offer in the city. This is not to be confused with food you would eat in mainland China, or even the Chinese food at restaurants here in the UK. Instead, Indo-Chinese is a whole new sub-cuisine created a couple of centuries ago when the first Chinese immigrants arrived and settled in what is now Kolkata. As the most easterly port in India, it provided the easiest access from China and people arrived there from all over the country. The largest of these communities were the Hakka and Cantonese, who were fleeing the civil war and conflict with Japan; Kolkata offered them a safe haven as well as new business opportunities.

According to British records at the time, a certain Tong Atchew was India's first Chinese immigrant in 1778. He set up a sugar mill in the city, providing employment for those who followed. Others became carpenters, tanners, dentists and laundrymen. They intermarried with the local population and completely immersed themselves in the city, learning the language and establishing two Chinatowns – Tiretta Bazar and Tangra – so that by the turn of twentieth century there were over 20,000 inhabitants of Chinese ancestry in Kolkata.

Initially, Chinese eating establishments were run by the Chinese for Chinese settlers, but they soon realised that opening their doors to a wider audience offered more opportunities. In order to appeal to their new customer base, Chinese cooks began to fuse their flavours with Indian ingredients. They introduced irresistibly sweet, sour, salty and spicy fusion dishes that would have been unrecognisable back in China, but that the local Indian community welcomed, and continue to enjoy, to this day.

Sadly, the Chinese community in Kolkata has greatly decreased in more recent years, to no more than a couple of thousand inhabitants. Their population declined steeply in the early 1960s during the Indo-China war which stemmed from a long-standing border dispute in the north of the country. China invaded India through Ladakh, resulting in significant loss of life on both sides, including the deaths of many Indian soldiers. In response, Chinese immigrants from Kolkata were placed in detention camps on the other side of the country in the state of Rajasthan. During this time many of the tanneries, which provided employment to so many, were shut down by the government without warning, depriving the Bengali Chinese of their livelihoods. After their release, many decided to move overseas, particularly to the US, Canada and Australia. Today, the younger Chinese generations in Bengal, like their Indian counterparts, often move abroad to further their studies and many end up not returning after their education. Perhaps the booming economies across India will reverse this trend over the next couple of decades.

When I visit Kolkata, I always like to walk around the remaining Indo-Chinese neighbourhoods, with their Taoist temples and sellers offering all manner of dumplings and Hakka noodles from their street stalls. For me, Indo-Chinese food is a complete delight – not only thanks to its irresistible flavours but also because of how easily it can be recreated at home, as I hope you'll discover through the recipes in this chapter.

Chilli Chicken

Preparation time: 25 minutes
Cooking time: 30 minutes
Serves 4-6

For the marinated chicken

800g boneless chicken thighs or breast, cut into 1-inch cubes

190g buttermilk (or 125g milk + 65g full-fat yoghurt)

1 egg, whisked

1 tsp fine salt

For the coating

180g plain flour

60g cornflour

2 tsp garlic powder

1 tsp ground white pepper

½ tsp mustard powder

½ tsp ground ginger

1 tsp fine salt

For the sauce

2 tbsp tomato ketchup

2 tbsp dark or light soy sauce

1 tbsp Shaoxing rice wine

1 tbsp Chinese black rice vinegar (also known as Chinkiang)

1 tbsp sriracha

1 egg

1 tsp freshly ground black pepper

½ tsp MSG (optional – see notes)

150ml chicken stock (½ a stock cube)

For the pan

Vegetable or sunflower oil, for frying

2 tbsp vegetable, sunflower or rapeseed oil

1 tbsp ginger-garlic paste

1 small or medium red onion

1 red, green or yellow bell pepper

2-3 fresh green chillies, halved lengthways (optional)

3 spring onions, finely sliced

White or black sesame seeds, to serve

Indo-Chinese chilli chicken was one of the first dishes to win over the hearts and minds of the Indian Bengali community in Kolkata when Chinese immigrants settled in the city back in the eighteenth century and began to open street stalls offering snacks to passersby, some of which later developed into restaurants. The Chinese immigrants wanted to appeal to their new customer base, having originally only prepared food for their own community. They began to meld Chinese flavours with Indian ingredients, creating irresistibly sweet, sour, salty and spicy fusion recipes which would have been unrecognisable back in China.

1. Begin by making the marinade. Combine the buttermilk (or milk and yoghurt), egg and salt in a large bowl, add the chicken and mix well to coat all the pieces. Cover and leave in the fridge while you prepare the other ingredients.

2. In a separate bowl, combine the flour and cornflour with the garlic, white pepper, mustard, ginger and salt. Mix well and set aside.

3. In a third bowl, combine all the ingredients for the sauce, mix well and set aside. Now prepare all the ingredients for the pan. Quarter the onion and separate the layers into petals, then slice the bell pepper into similar size pieces.

4. Using a medium saucepan or deep frying pan, pour in the oil for frying until it reaches halfway up the side. Heat the oil to approximately 177°C/350°F. I always use the ring at the back of the hob for safety reasons. Check the temperature with an oil thermometer or drop a pinch of flour into the oil, which should hiss immediately. If the oil is not hot enough, the chicken will end up soggy.

5. While the oil is heating up, remove the chicken from the fridge. Pour a few tablespoons of the marinade into the flour coating and use your fingers to mix. It won't form a batter but the clumps will create extra crunch on the chicken when deep fried.

6. Place a few of the chicken pieces into the coating and toss to cover them completely. Use tongs or a spider strainer to gently lower the chicken into the oil. It needs to be cooked in small batches to fry evenly, and remember that the oil temperature will drop once you add the chicken so monitor the heat to ensure it cooks as evenly as possible.

7. The chicken will take about 5 minutes per batch to fry and should be nicely bronzed all over. Move it around a couple of times while frying and then transfer to a plate lined with kitchen paper to drain once crisp and cooked through. Repeat with all the chicken.

8. Finally, heat a wok or wide pan. Add the 2 tablespoons of oil and when hot, add the ginger-garlic paste followed by the red onion, bell pepper and chillies, if using.

9. After 3 to 4 minutes, add the prepared sauce and allow it to bubble for 3 to 5 minutes. This should help it thicken and reduce slightly but if you want the sauce even thicker, mix a little cornflour with cold water to make a paste and then stir this into the pan.

10. Just before serving, add the crispy fried chicken pieces and mix well to coat them in the sauce. Scatter with the spring onions and sesame seeds, then serve immediately with plain basmati rice.

Hakka Chilli Paneer

Preparation time: 10 minutes
Cooking time: 15-20 minutes
Serves 4

450g paneer, cut into ½-inch cubes

3 tsp cornflour

¼ tsp ground white or black pepper

4 tbsp sunflower or vegetable oil, for frying

For the chilli sauce

2 tbsp vegetable, sunflower or rapeseed oil

1 red onion, roughly chopped

4 garlic cloves, finely chopped

1-2 fresh red or green chillies, finely sliced (optional)

2 tbsp tomato ketchup

2 tbsp dark soy sauce

1 lime, juiced

1 tsp brown sugar

½ tsp Kashmiri chilli powder

½ a bell pepper, cut into 1-inch pieces (optional)

3 spring onions, finely sliced

Handful of fresh coriander, finely chopped

1 tsp sesame oil

1 tsp white sesame seeds, to serve

What could be more irresistible than cubes of crispy paneer coated in a sweet, sticky chilli sauce? This Indo-Chinese classic is much loved in Kolkata and is always part of any feast.

1. In a bowl, lightly dust the cubed paneer with the cornflour and ground pepper.

2. Heat the oil in a wok, kadai or frying pan and when hot, fry the paneer until crispy and bronzed on one or two sides. Do this in batches, removing the paneer with a slotted spoon and draining on kitchen paper as you go.

3. Using the same pan for the sauce, add a little more oil if required, then add the onion, garlic and fresh chilli, if using. Cook on a medium to high heat for 2 to 3 minutes, moving them around the pan, before adding the tomato ketchup and dark soy sauce.

4. Add the lime juice, brown sugar and Kashmiri chilli powder to the sauce along with a little water if it needs loosening. Stir well to make sure everything is incorporated.

5. Return the crispy paneer to the pan and fold in so the sauce clings to the paneer. If you are using bell pepper, add this now along with the spring onion.

6. Cook while stirring gently for 2 to 3 minutes before adding the fresh coriander and sesame oil. Finally, sprinkle with the white sesame seeds to serve.

Notes: This recipe is best made fresh and eaten immediately rather than cooked in advance. It's great with the Sichuan Fried Rice on page 22.

Sichuan Fried Rice

Preparation time: 10 minutes
Cooking time: 15 minutes
Serves 4

150g basmati rice (or 4 handfuls)

500ml cold water

2 tbsp vegetable, sunflower or
rapeseed oil

1 large carrot, finely chopped into small
cubes

200g fine green beans, finely chopped

2 spring onions, finely chopped and
separated into green and white parts

½ red bell pepper, finely diced
(optional)

2 tbsp Sichuan chilli sauce (store-
bought or homemade – see page 44)

25ml water

1 tsp sesame oil

Salt, to taste

Although the recipe below uses rice cooked from scratch, this is also a great way
to use up leftover rice. If you have made my Sichuan Chilli Sauce (see page 44),
then this is a great recipe to include it – though you can of course use store-
bought sauce.

1. Begin by gently washing your rice, being careful not to break up the grains. To
    do this, place it in the pan you intend to cook it in and cover with cold water.
    Gently move the rice around the pan with your hand in a circular motion. Pour
    out the water and repeat.

2. Cover the rice with the 500ml of cold water. Bring to the boil and then simmer
    on a low heat for 10 minutes. After this time, the rice should be perfectly
    cooked – test some to check. Drain the rice and then briefly rinse with cold
    water to stop it cooking further and sticking together. Turn out onto a large
    plate or tray and leave the rice to dry out.

3. While the rice is cooking, heat a wok or cast-iron pan and add the oil.
    Immediately add the carrots, green beans, the white part of the spring onion
    and the bell pepper, if using. Stir fry for 3 minutes on a medium to high heat
    and then add the Sichuan chilli sauce and the water. Cook while stirring for a
    couple more minutes so that all the ingredients are fully coated and sufficiently
    softened in the sauce.

4. Add salt to taste and check the seasoning. Drizzle over the sesame oil and mix
    into the sauce. Turn off the heat and then spoon the cooled rice into the pan,
    folding it into the sauce and vegetables.

5. Turn the heat back on for a further minute or two and stir until everything is
    combined and the rice is hot. Finally, add the spring onion greens and serve
    immediately.

Sweetcorn Soup with Chilli Vinegar

Preparation time: 5 minutes
Cooking time: 10 minutes
Serves 4-6

This delicious Indo-Chinese staple has thin shreds of egg running through the soup, hence the name it can also be referred to by: egg drop soup. The chilli vinegar dressing gives it that extra kick and the whole dish only takes minutes to prepare and cook – perfect when you are after a nourishing meal quickly.

For the dressing

2 fresh chillies, finely sliced

4 tbsp rice wine vinegar

1 tsp caster sugar

For the soup

1.3 litres vegetable or chicken stock

400g fresh, frozen or tinned sweetcorn

2 eggs

3 tbsp cornflour

5 tbsp cold water

½ tsp ground white pepper, or to taste

1 tsp fine salt, or to taste

2 spring onions, finely sliced

1 tsp light soy sauce per serving

1 tsp sesame oil per serving

1. Begin by placing the chillies, vinegar and sugar in a small bowl. Mix well to dissolve the sugar and then set aside.

2. Heat the stock in a pan, then add the sweetcorn and simmer gently for 5 minutes. Use a handheld blender to partially blend the soup, leaving some of the sweetcorn whole to add texture.

3. Crack the eggs into a small bowl, whisk and then set aside. In a separate small bowl, mix the cornflour and cold water into a smooth watery paste, then stir this into the soup. The cornflour paste will help the soup to thicken as it simmers.

4. After 3 minutes, add the white pepper and salt, then stir in half the spring onions. Bring the soup to the boil and skim any scum off the surface.

5. Now take the soup off the heat. This is an important step to avoid the egg being scrambled. Gradually pour the whisked egg into the soup, gently stirring with a chopstick. Wispy threads should form in the soup as you stir.

6. To serve, ladle the soup into bowls and drizzle a couple of teaspoons (or more if you wish) of the chilli vinegar dressing over each portion, along with the soy sauce, sesame oil and a sprinkling of spring onion. Gently stir in and then slurp away.

Notes: If you want to bulk out the soup, you can add half a chicken breast, very finely sliced or chopped, along with the sweetcorn in Step 2.

Chicken Momo

Preparation time: I hour
Cooking time: 14 minutes
Makes 27

For the wrappers

180g plain flour

60g cornflour

I tsp fine salt

2 tsp vegetable, sunflower or rapeseed oil

130ml warm water

OR about 30 store-bought wrappers

For the filling

300g chicken mince, or 2 small chicken breasts (see Step 3)

½ a medium onion, finely minced

2 spring onions, finely sliced

4 garlic cloves, finely grated

I tbsp finely grated fresh ginger

1-2 fresh green chillies, finely chopped (optional)

3 tbsp finely chopped fresh coriander, leaves and stalks

2 tbsp light soy sauce

I tsp freshly ground black pepper

½ tsp fine salt

Pinch of MSG (optional)

If you are visiting Kolkata and are an early riser, I urge you to head to Tiretta Bazaar, the oldest of the two Chinatowns in Kolkata. Sadly, the number of Chinese residents in the city is dwindling, but there are still several stalls selling breakfast delights to punters. I always make a beeline for this neighbourhood when I am visiting relatives in the city. Momos, which are dumplings, are a must, and they are often served on little paper plates with a hot sauce or chilli oil on the side. If you fancy making your own to accompany these momos, see my recipes on pages 176 and 46.

1. To make the wrappers, sift both flours into a bowl, then add the salt and half the oil. Mix well, then gradually add the warm water until the mixture comes together into a dough.

2. Turn out the dough onto a clean surface and knead it for 3 to 5 minutes. Shape into a ball, coat with the remaining teaspoon of oil, then place back in the bowl and cover with a damp cloth while you make the filling.

3. If you are mincing your own chicken, I suggest using a Magimix or equivalent blender and then adding all the other ingredients for the filling to blitz until combined. If you have bought chicken mince, then you can combine all the ingredients yourself in a bowl, although I find using a blender is the best way to bring everything together.

4. Take 13g of the dough and roll out to form a disc 4 inches in diameter and no thicker than a penny. You can use an upturned glass or a cookie cutter to cut out the rounds. I make each momo one at a time, keeping the uncut dough covered to stop it drying out.

5. Place I heaped teaspoon of the filling into the centre of the wrapper. You now have 4 options for shaping the momo, which are all easy to achieve.

(Continued overleaf...)

Chicken Momo (Continued)

Option 1

Bring the bottom half of the wrapper up towards the top half of the wrapper, enclosing the filling. You can then gently press the opposite sides of the dough together to create a half-moon shape. Once a half-moon has been created, take both corners and bring them round so they meet at the bottom and then slightly cross over, like a tortellini. These dumplings are also known as rosebuds.

Option 2

This method makes a three-pointed momo. Place a teaspoon of filling into the centre of the wrapper and then squeeze the dough together a third of the way up at one end. Then bring the middle of the open part of the wrapper up to the central crease, making a triangle shape with 3 corners. Secure the edges firmly.

Option 3

Start bringing one side of the wrapper up in a pleating motion as if you are bunching the wrapper together. Keep turning, pleating as you go and enclosing the filling until you have run out of dough and created a round momo with a pleated top.

1. Momo can be steamed, fried or boiled, but my preference is to steam them. If you are using a metal steamer, oil the bottom to make it non-stick. If you are using a bamboo steamer, cut out rounds of baking parchment to fit the base.

2. Add water to the steamer and bring to the boil. Place your momos in the steamer, cover with the lid and steam for 14 to 15 minutes.

3. To fry the momo, simply add a little oil to a pan with a well-fitting lid and then place the momos in the pan. Allow the bottom of the momos to lightly bronze over a couple of minutes, then add about 50ml of water and cover with the lid to allow it to steam for 4 to 6 minutes, by which time the water will have been absorbed. Try one momo to check the dough is cooked through and steam for a few more minutes if required.

4. To boil the momo, I like to have a vegetable, miso or chicken stock on hand for extra flavour. Add the momo to the hot stock and cook on a medium to low heat for 10 to 15 minutes. You can also cook them from frozen with this method.

5. Serve your momo alongside Himalayan Hot Sauce (see page 176) or homemade chilli oil (see page 46) or simply with soy sauce for dipping into before eating.

Notes: You can replace the chicken mince with pork mince if you prefer. The momo wrappers can be made with 240g of plain flour but I think they taste much better with the cornflour. The wrappers can be frozen, lightly floured so they don't stick together and stored in an airtight freezer bag. You can also freeze the filled momos by placing them on a tray in the freezer for 1 hour and then transferring them to a freezer bag or airtight container for storing.

Fish Ball Soup

Preparation time: 20 minutes
Cooking time: 7 minutes
Serves 4 (makes 20 fish balls)

While this recipe might not sound the most exciting, it creates a delicate yet comforting soup with a light flavour profile that's great for autumn or winter months in the UK when there is a chill in the air. If you're feeling under the weather, this will definitely give you an inner glow.

For the fish balls

360g mackerel fillets

2 garlic cloves, minced

½ tsp ground white pepper

1 tsp salt

1 egg white

1 tbsp cornstarch

30ml ice-cold water (approximately)

For the stock

1.5 litres fish stock (2 stock or bouillon cubes)

2-inch piece (30g) of fresh ginger, finely sliced into batons

½ tsp ground white pepper

½ tsp fine salt

½ tsp caster sugar

2 tbsp light soy sauce

1 spring onion, finely sliced

1 tbsp finely chopped fresh coriander stalks

1 tbsp chopped fresh coriander leaves, to serve

For the garnish

3 banana shallots, finely sliced

2 tbsp vegetable, sunflower or rapeseed oil

OR

Handful of store-bought crispy shallots

1. Skin the mackerel fillets, using a spoon to help scrape the flesh from the skins. You should be left with approximately 280g of mackerel flesh. Discard the skins and place the flesh in a bowl.

2. Add the minced garlic, white pepper, salt, egg white and cornstarch to the mackerel and mix well using a spoon or your hand. Slowly add the cold water until the mixture comes together smoothly. If you have a stand mixer, whisk on a low speed for 5 minutes while gradually adding the cold water – this makes the texture super smooth.

3. Fill a separate bowl with ice-cold water and place it next to your mackerel mixture. Use a teaspoon to scoop up some of the mixture and drop it into the bowl of iced water. Alternatively, take some of the mixture in your hand and squeeze it through your thumb and first finger so that a rough ball forms. Use a spoon to scoop away the ball and drop it into the bowl. They don't need to be too neat; the more rustic and homestyle the better!

4. Once all the fish balls are made and resting in the iced water, make the garnish (unless you are using store-bought crispy shallots). Shallow fry the sliced shallots in the oil until they are bronzed and crispy. Remove with a slotted spoon and place on kitchen paper.

5. Place the fish stock in a deep pan along with the ginger batons, white pepper, salt, caster sugar and light soy sauce. Bring to a high simmer for 4 minutes. Taste the broth to see if it needs any more seasoning.

6. Add half the spring onion and all the coriander stalks to the broth. Gently add the fish balls and simmer for 3 minutes, until all the balls have risen to the top of the soup. They should be soft and tender.

7. Ladle the soup into bowls and sprinkle the remaining spring onions, coriander leaves and crispy shallots on top.

Notes: If you want to make this light soup into a more filling meal, you can add a nest of rice noodles per serving. If you're not a fan of mackerel, it can be replaced with cod.

Gobi Manchurian

Preparation time: 20 minutes
Cooking time: 20 minutes
Serves 4

1 small or medium whole cauliflower, florets only

150g self-raising flour, or plain flour + 1 tsp baking powder

80g cornflour

½ tsp Kashmiri chilli powder

½ tsp fine salt

280ml water

Vegetable or sunflower oil, for frying

For the sauce

1 tbsp sesame oil

1 tbsp vegetable oil

1 tbsp finely grated fresh ginger

1 tbsp finely chopped or grated garlic

½ red onion, finely chopped

5 spring onions, finely sliced

2 fresh green chillies, finely sliced (optional)

3 tbsp soy sauce

2 tbsp Sichuan chilli sauce (see page 44) or sriracha

2 tbsp white or black vinegar

2 tbsp tomato ketchup

1 tsp honey, maple syrup or fine brown sugar

1 tsp cornflour

2 tbsp water

To serve

1 tbsp white sesame seeds

2 spring onions, finely sliced

Small handful of fresh coriander

Gobi (cauliflower) Manchurian is an absolute cracker of a dish, offering spicy, tangy and sweet notes. It was reportedly invented by Nelson Wang, an Indian restaurateur of Chinese descent who was originally from Kolkata but moved to Mumbai in the 1970s to become a chef. He came up with the idea of Chicken Manchurian when he fed the president of BCCI and Cricket Club India and his guests; the fusion of Indian spices with Chinese ingredients wowed the diners. Replacing the chicken with cauliflower was the next step, with both dishes becoming a mainstay in every Chinese restaurant in India and beyond, including *China Garden* which Wang went on to establish in Mumbai.

1. Begin by removing the stalks and leaves from the cauliflower (save these to use up in another recipe). Cut the cauliflower into small or medium florets of equal size.

2. Blanch the cauliflower florets in boiling water for 2 to 3 minutes, then drain immediately and pat dry with kitchen paper.

3. In a bowl, combine the flour, cornflour, Kashmiri chilli powder and salt with the water, whisking until you have a smooth batter. It should be thick enough to coat the cauliflower without running off.

4. Heat an inch of vegetable or sunflower oil in a frying pan. Add a droplet of batter to check the temperature – when the oil is hot enough, the batter will sizzle on the surface.

5. Place a few of the cauliflower florets in the batter and cover them completely. Carefully place them into the oil with tongs. Fry until golden brown, which will take around 3 minutes, then remove and place on kitchen paper to drain.

6. Continue to coat and cook the cauliflower in batches, making sure the pan doesn't become too full and keeping the temperature of the oil constant. When the frying is done, let the oil cool completely before straining and bottling it to be reused.

7. To make the sauce, heat the oils in a wok or frying pan, then add the ginger, garlic and onion. Stir for a couple of minutes to soften.

8. Add the spring onions and fresh green chillies, if using, to the pan and after 30 seconds, add the soy sauce, chilli sauce, vinegar, tomato ketchup and honey, maple syrup or brown sugar. Stir to combine everything thoroughly.

9. Mix the cornflour and water in a small bowl to make a paste, then add this to the pan while stirring constantly to thicken the sauce slightly. Add an extra splash of water at this stage if it looks too dry.

10. Taste the sauce to check the seasoning. Because it includes soy sauce you probably won't need extra salt.

11. Finally, gently fold the crispy cauliflower into the sauce. Scatter with the sesame seeds, spring onions and fresh coriander, then serve immediately while the cauliflower is crisp.

Notes: For true crispiness, frying is best for this recipe. You could bake or air fry the battered cauliflower, but it won't achieve the same texture as frying.

Manchow Soup

Preparation time: 10-15 minutes
Cooking time: 10-15 minutes
Serves 8 as a starter or 4 if using larger bowls

Manchow soup is another classic Indo-Chinese dish that was invented on Indian soil by Chinese immigrants. The 'chow' refers to crispy noodles that sit on top of the soup, adding crunch for an extra textural dimension. The soup is full of flavour and guaranteed to warm you up throughout the winter months.

For the crispy noodles

2 nests of egg noodles

1-2 tsp cornflour

2 tbsp vegetable, sunflower or rapeseed oil

For the soup

2 tbsp vegetable oil

1 tbsp finely grated garlic

1 tbsp finely grated fresh ginger

1 green chilli, slit lengthways

2 spring onions, finely sliced

2 large carrots, finely diced

100g green beans, finely sliced

10 button mushrooms, finely diced

2 tbsp finely sliced coriander stalks

1.5 litres vegetable stock (2 stock or bouillon cubes)

¼ tsp freshly ground black pepper

¼ tsp ground white pepper

Pinch of MSG (optional)

2 tbsp soy sauce

1 tbsp white or rice vinegar

1 tbsp tomato ketchup

1 tsp red chilli sauce (such as sriracha)

½ tsp fine salt

2 tbsp cornflour

4 tbsp cold water

Fresh coriander, chopped

1. Begin by preparing the crispy noodles. Boil them according to the packet instructions – usually 3 or 4 minutes – then drain and spread out on a sheet of baking paper to dry.

2. Once dry, dust the noodles with the cornflour and use your hands to toss and coat them. They may be a little sticky to begin with, but the cornflour will help separate them as well as ensuring they crisp up in the next step.

3. Heat the oil in a frying pan and add a handful of the noodles so that they don't overcrowd the pan. After a minute, use tongs to turn them over. They will begin to lightly bronze and crisp up. Remove and place on kitchen paper to soak up the excess oil and then repeat until all the noodles are crispy.

4. Prepare all the ingredients for the soup, making sure you have everything to hand as once you get started, it comes together quickly.

5. Heat the vegetable oil in a deep pan and then add the garlic, ginger and green chilli. Move them around the pan for a minute and then add all the other vegetables, including the coriander stalks. Continue to stir so they do not catch on the bottom.

6. After 1 to 2 minutes, add the vegetable stock and bring to the boil, then simmer for 7 minutes. Add the black and white pepper, MSG, soy sauce, vinegar, tomato ketchup, chilli sauce and salt.

7. In a small bowl, mix the cornflour with the cold water to form a smooth paste. Add this to the pan and stir well. Allow the soup to thicken over the next couple of minutes. If you are looking for a thicker soup, add half the amount of cornflour paste again.

8. Taste the soup to check the seasoning and adjust as needed. Ladle into bowls and top with the crispy noodles and fresh coriander to serve.

Notes: The crispy noodles can be made in advance and then stored in an airtight container until needed. The soup can also be made in advance and then reheated before serving. It's very versatile as you can easily add a wide range of vegetables. A handful of finely sliced white or red cabbage works well and can be added instead of, or in addition to, any of the above vegetables. The MSG can be left out but is a great flavour enhancer – see notes on page 15.

Savoury Steamed Buns

Preparation time: 45-50 minutes
Cooking time: 20-25 minutes
Makes 12

For the dough

1 tsp easy bake/instant yeast or active dry yeast

1 tsp caster sugar

20ml warm water

250g plain white flour

140ml warm water

1 tsp fine salt

For the filling

300g minced meat, crumbled paneer or firm tofu, or mushrooms

2 Chinese chives, finely sliced or 4 Western chives, finely chopped

2 spring onions, finely sliced

1 tsp finely grated fresh ginger

1 tbsp oyster sauce (or hoisin for vegan buns)

1 tbsp sesame oil

1 tbsp light soy sauce

1 tbsp Shaoxing rice wine

2 tsp cornflour

1 tsp fine salt

½ tsp caster sugar

¼ tsp ground white pepper

Wandering around Tiretta Bazaar, Kolkata's oldest and original Chinatown, in the early morning on a Sunday is a culinary delight, as Indo-Chinese residents set up their food stalls and steam begins to rise. Passersby wait in earnest for the stalls to open so feasting can commence. Bao buns are a regular sight, often filled with char sui (Chinese barbecue pork) or vegetarian options like mushrooms and bok choy. This is my version, which you can fill with any minced meat, crumbled paneer or tofu, or a variety of vegetables – all are equally delicious.

To make the dough and filling

1. If you are using easy bake/instant yeast, skip this step. If you are using active dry yeast, place it in a small bowl along with the caster sugar and add the 20ml of warm water. Mix well, then cover and set aside for 10 minutes to allow it to activate. Small bubbles will come to the surface, and it will begin to look frothy.

2. You can make the dough by hand in a large bowl, or in a stand mixer. Sift the flour into the bowl or mixer and add the salt. Stir well, then pour in the activated yeast or add the easy bake/instant yeast and use a chopstick to mix in a circular motion.

3. Gradually add the 140ml of warm water as you mix the ingredients gently, allowing the flour to bind and form a dough ball. If you feel it needs a little more water, add in very small amounts. If the dough feels too wet, add a little more flour.

4. If you are making the dough by hand, lift it out once it has come together and knead on a clean surface for 10 minutes until it feels very soft and bounces back slightly when you poke it with your finger. In a stand mixer, use the dough hook attachment on a low speed (2 works well on my KitchenAid) for 7 minutes.

5. Return the dough to the bowl, rub some neutral oil on your hands and pat the dough all over to stop it drying out. Cover the bowl with clingfilm or a clean, damp cloth and then leave the dough in a warm place to double in size for 1 hour 30 minutes (see notes).

6. While the dough is resting, prepare the filling. Combine all the ingredients, stirring in a circular motion until the mixture is soft.

(Continued overleaf...)

Savoury Steamed Buns (Continued)

To stuff and steam the buns

1. If you are using a bamboo steamer, cut out rounds of baking paper for the individual buns to sit on, or one large round with little holes in to allow the steam through. Place these at the bottom of your steamer trays. If you are using a metal steamer, lightly oil the bottom of your steamer trays with neutral oil.

2. Return to your dough, which will have now doubled in size. Cut in half and place half back in the bowl, covered. Knead the other half for a couple of minutes and then roll it into a long sausage shape and cut into 6 pieces about the size of a golf ball.

3. Sprinkle a little flour on your work surface and then take one dough ball, leaving the rest under a damp tea towel. Flatten the ball with the palm of your hand to form a disc, then roll out a little with a rolling pin. Continue rolling around the edge of the disc, using one hand to roll and the other to turn the dough slightly. You are aiming to make the edges slightly thinner than the centre and the disc to be approximately 4.5 inches in diameter.

4. Spoon 1 to 2 teaspoons of filling into the centre of the dough and then use your thumb and forefinger to make small pleats, folding the dough up into the centre and working your way round until no filling is showing. Alternatively, you can simply bring the dough up around the filling to cover completely without pleating, then twist at the tip and remove any excess dough. They will become neater with practice. Place the filled buns on the baking paper, if using a bamboo steamer, or straight into the oiled metal steamer and continue until they are all ready to steam.

5. Add water to your steamer and bring to the boil, making sure it's not too full so that no water touches the dough. Steam the buns for 15 minutes.

6. After steaming, turn off the heat and leave the lid on the pan for a further 5 minutes. Once rested, the buns are ready to eat. They are very tasty with Himalayan Hot Sauce (see page 176) or a mixture of light soy sauce, Shaoxing and chilli sauce for dipping.

Notes: For a veggie bun, mushrooms have a good texture which is why I've suggested them above, but you could use finely sliced cabbage, celery, carrots or almost any other vegetable you like in the filling. For minced meat, pork, beef and chicken all work well – I use the chopper setting on my Magimix to make my own chicken mince.

These buns can be made ahead and then frozen. Once filled and sealed, place the buns on a baking tray to freeze, then transfer to a resealable bag and store in the freezer. Cook them from frozen in your steamer for 20 minutes and then let them rest for 5 minutes with the lid on.

When proving dough, I always pop the oven on a low heat for 5 minutes and then turn it off completely, keeping the oven door slightly ajar and the light switched on. I then place the covered bowl of dough in the warm oven to prove until it rises. If you live in a warm climate, simply leave the covered dough to one side and it will prove at room temperature.

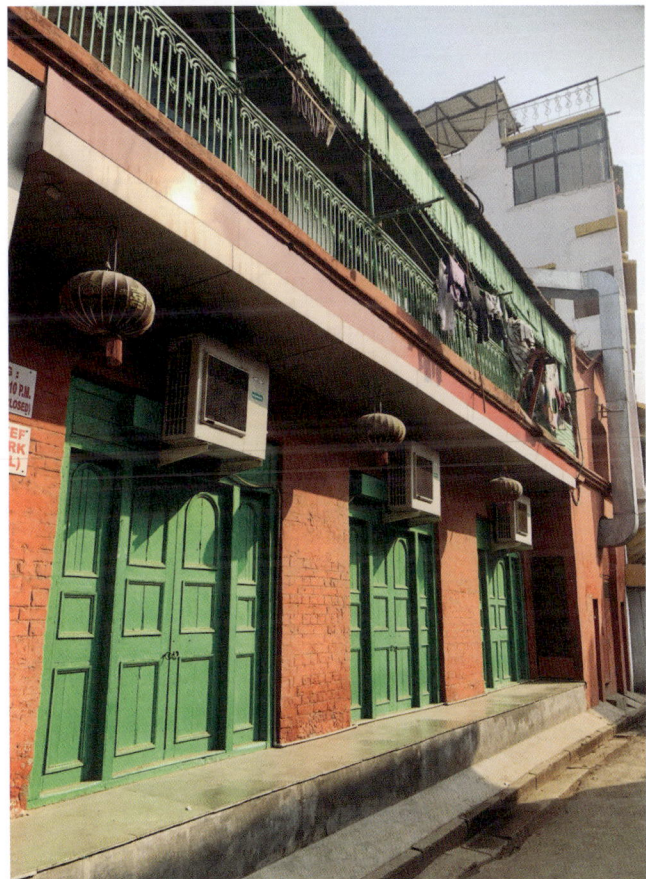

Veggie Hakka Noodles

Preparation time: 10-15 minutes
Cooking time: 10 minutes
Serves 4

4 nests of egg noodles

2 tbsp vegetable, sunflower or rapeseed oil

2 eggs

1 red onion, cut into thin half moons

½ tsp fine salt

3 garlic cloves, finely chopped

2 fresh green chillies, finely chopped

1-inch piece (15g) of fresh ginger, finely grated

½ a large carrot, cut into matchsticks

¼ white cabbage, finely sliced

4 tbsp soy sauce

2 tbsp sriracha sauce

2 tsp green chilli sauce

1 tbsp rice vinegar

1 tsp brown or caster sugar

Freshly ground black pepper, to taste

½ tsp garam masala

1 spring onion, finely sliced

1 lime, juiced

In the late eighteenth century, a community known as the Hakkas, originally from South China, migrated to Kolkata. In Cantonese, the word hakka means 'guest people'. Using the ingredients available to them, these settlers began to create their own unique style of Chinese food which over the centuries has morphed into an array of popular dishes throughout India and beyond. Hakka noodles, the Indo-Chinese version of chow mein, is one of most loved.

1. Cook the egg noodles in boiling water according to the packet instructions – usually around 3 minutes – or until soft. Drain in a sieve and run under cold water before placing in a bowl with a teaspoon of the oil and gently coating the noodles. This will prevent them from sticking.

2. Break the eggs into a small bowl and whisk with a fork. Now heat a wide, deep pan – a wok would work well here. Add a teaspoon of the oil and pour in the whisked eggs. Push them around the pan as they cook to break up but not scramble the eggs. After 30 seconds, remove them from the pan and place in a clean bowl.

3. Using the same pan, heat the remaining oil and when hot, add three quarters of the red onion with the salt (this will speed up the cooking of the onions).

4. After 3 minutes, add the garlic, green chilli, ginger and carrot sticks. Move everything around the pan for another minute before adding the white cabbage. Continue to stir gently for a further couple of minutes.

5. In a small bowl, combine all the sauces with the vinegar and sugar. Mix well.

6. Add the noodles and egg to the pan and gently mix with the vegetables. Now add the sauce, black pepper and garam masala. Toss gently and then transfer to a large bowl.

7. Top with the spring onions and remaining red onion, then squeeze over the lime juice and serve.

Notes: Other vegetables that work well here include bell peppers, mushrooms and cauliflower. Sometimes I like to swap out black pepper with Sichuan pepper for that extra tingling sensation.

Sichuan Chilli Honey Roasties

Preparation time: 15 minutes
Cooking time: 40 minutes
Serves 4

700g mini roasting potatoes or new potatoes, skin on and kept whole

3 tbsp olive oil

2 tbsp vegetable or sunflower oil

4 garlic cloves, finely chopped

1-inch piece (15g) of fresh ginger, finely chopped

2 dried whole red chillies

½ tsp freshly ground black pepper

½ tsp chilli flakes

3 tsp light soy sauce

1 tbsp Sichuan chilli sauce (store-bought or homemade, see page 44), sriracha or red chilli sauce

1 tbsp tomato purée

1 tbsp runny honey

2 tbsp water

1 spring onion, green part only finely sliced + 1 extra to serve

1 tsp white sesame seeds, plus extra to serve

This recipe is a healthier twist on the fried potatoes you can find in the Indo-Chinese restaurants in Kolkata and can be made in an air fryer instead of the oven if you like. You can buy store-bought Sichuan sauce, which is found at most large supermarkets, or make your own with the recipe on page 44 which requires sourcing Sichuan peppercorns (see page 13).

1. Place the potatoes in a pan of water and parboil for 10 minutes. Drain thoroughly, then spread out in a roasting tray and use kitchen paper to pat dry.

2. Pour the olive oil over the potatoes and mix well. Place in a preheated oven at 200°C/180°C fan/400°F/Gas 6 for 35 to 40 minutes.

3. Meanwhile, heat the vegetable or sunflower oil in a wide pan and then add the garlic and ginger. Stir for 2 minutes before adding the dried chillies, black pepper, chilli flakes, soy sauce, chilli sauce, tomato purée and runny honey. Mix well and then add the water. Simmer for a couple of minutes and then take the pan off the heat.

4. When the potatoes are nicely roasted, remove them from the oven and transfer to a mixing bowl. Pour the sauce over the potatoes and toss together. Add the spring onion and white sesame seeds, then mix well.

5. Transfer them to a serving bowl and sprinkle with the remaining spring onions and white sesame seeds.

Notes: If you have an air fryer, you can cook the potatoes at 190°C for about 15 minutes. There's no need to parboil them first BUT it is important to leave them in a bowl of room temperature water for an hour before draining and drying them completely. This will help remove the starch and ensure they are not soggy when air frying. Make sure they are bite-size and cook in a single layer. Give them a good shake at 8 minutes and then check on them again at 15 minutes. Use a knife to check they are cooked all the way through. If they require a little longer, check on them at 2-minute intervals. If you want a little extra kick in the sauce, I recommend replacing the runny honey with WilderBee hot honey which adds a lovely sweet heat.

Sichuan Chilli Sauce

Preparation time: 15 minutes
Cooking time: 10 minutes
Makes 1 jar

25 dried Kashmiri chillies (you can use a hot dried chilli variety instead, if you prefer extra heat)

4 tbsp water

1 tbsp sesame oil

3 tbsp vegetable, sunflower or rapeseed oil

15 garlic cloves, finely grated or blended until smooth

2-inch piece (30g) of fresh ginger, finely grated or blended until smooth

1 tsp Sichuan peppercorns, crushed

3 tbsp rice or cider vinegar

2 tbsp tomato ketchup

1 tsp tomato paste

1 tbsp soy sauce

1 tbsp honey, maple syrup or fine brown sugar

½ tsp fine salt

Making your own Sichuan chilli sauce will always be superior to shop-bought, as you can tailor it to suit your personal taste. As the name suggests, Sichuan peppercorns are a key ingredient. They are actually berries, from the prickly ash tree which is part of the citrus family, and have a deliciously zingy, sour flavour which dances on the tip of your tongue and creates a numbing sensation – but in a good way! The first time I tasted them was in Hong Kong and they blew me away. I absolutely adore them and make sure they are always stocked in my pantry. They can easily be found online and at most Asian grocers (see page 244). In Kolkata, this sauce is also referred to as 'Szechuan Chutney'.

1. Place the dried chillies in a bowl, cover with hot water and leave for 10 minutes. They will puff up slightly and soften.

2. Drain the soaked chillies and then snip off the tops with scissors. Rinse them to allow some of the seeds to fall out. Almost all the heat of a chilli is in its seeds and membrane, so removing these will tone the heat level down.

3. Place the chillies in a blender, add the water and sesame oil, then blitz to form a smooth paste.

4. Heat the oil in a pan on a low heat, then add the garlic and ginger. Move them around the pan to cook until the raw smell has gone, then after 30 seconds add the crushed Sichuan peppercorns. Mix well.

5. Add the blended chilli paste, vinegar, tomato ketchup, tomato paste, soy sauce, honey, maple syrup or brown sugar and salt. Simmer on a gentle heat to let all the flavours infuse. If it sticks to the bottom of the pan, add a splash of water to loosen.

6. When you see oil come to the surface, the sauce is ready. Decant into a sterilised jar and seal. Store for 1 to 2 months and once opened, store in the refrigerator.

Notes: This versatile recipe is used in my Sichuan Fried Rice on page 22 and my Sichuan Chilli Honey Roasties on page 42. It's also great with the Veggie Hakka Noodles on page 40 and Gobi Manchurian on page 32 and is delicious alongside both varieties of the steamed buns (pages 36 and 160) and momo (pages 26 and 172) in this book as a dipping sauce.

Chilli Oil

Preparation time: 5 minutes
Makes 100ml

2 tsp chilli flakes

½ tsp Sichuan chilli flakes, crushed

2 tsp white sesame seeds

½ tsp finely chopped garlic

45ml sunflower, vegetable or rapeseed oil

2 tbsp light soy sauce

1 tsp caster sugar

1 tsp Chinkiang or rice vinegar

1 tbsp water

Pinch of salt

This chilli oil is the perfect accompaniment to many recipes in the Indo-Chinese and Tibetan Nepalese chapters, particularly the momos and noodle dishes. At street food stalls, similar chilli oils to this one are drizzled over momos for a delicious on-the-go snack.

1. Place both types of chilli flakes into a heatproof bowl with the white sesame seeds and finely chopped garlic. Mix well.

2. Heat the oil and when hot, pour it over the ingredients in the bowl. They will immediately begin to sizzle.

3. Stir in the light soy sauce, caster sugar, vinegar and water. Once cooled, taste the oil and add a pinch of salt if required.

4. Store in a sealed glass jar. Serve alongside the Chicken or Vegetable Momo on pages 26 and 172, the Savoury Steamed Buns on page 36 and Veggie Hakka Noodles on page 40. It also works well drizzled over Eggs on Okra (page 196).

Red Bean Sesame Balls

Preparation time: 20 minutes
Cooking time: 10 minutes
Makes 10

150g red bean paste

120g glutinous rice flour (see notes)

30g fine light brown sugar

¼ tsp fine salt

90ml boiling water

White sesame seeds

Vegetable or sunflower oil, for frying

These delicious mochi-style snacks are found in the Chinatowns of Kolkata. They are best eaten hot before the crispy outer shell starts to soften. Chewy and crispy with a nutty aroma from the sesame seed coating, they can also be found in mainland China and similar versions crop up in Japan and Vietnam.

1. Begin by rolling the red bean paste into 10 x 15g balls and placing these on a plate.

2. Next, add the flour, sugar and salt to a mixing bowl and stir well. Gradually pour in the boiling water and use a spatula to bring it all together, forming a ball of dough.

3. When it is cool enough to handle, portion the dough into 10 equal pieces and roll them into balls. Place these on a plate and cover with a damp cloth to stop them drying out.

4. Take one of the dough balls and flatten with the palm of your hand, then place a red bean ball in the middle. Bring the sides of the dough up to cover the red bean paste and then reshape to form a smooth round ball. It should be about the size of a golf ball.

5. Fill one small bowl with lukewarm water and another with raw white sesame seeds. Dip the filled ball briefly in the water and then roll in the sesame seeds until evenly coated. Gently roll the ball between the palms of your hands to allow the sesame seeds to properly stick to the dough. Repeat with the remaining red bean paste and dough balls.

6. Heat your smallest saucepan on a low heat with enough oil for deep frying. It is really important to heat the oil low and slow. When the oil is hot, drop in a sesame seed. If it sizzles immediately, the oil is the right temperature for frying. Add the sesame coated balls and as they begin to bronze, turn them over with a fork so they become evenly bronzed all over. This should take around 2 minutes in total.

7. Remove from the pan with a slotted spoon and drain briefly on kitchen paper to absorb excess oil and cool slightly. They are best eaten while still warm.

Notes: Glutinous rice flour is different from regular rice flour. It is a sweet rice flour made from sticky rice, as opposed to long or medium-grain rice, so the texture is far chewier when made into a dough.

Anglo-Indian

Over the 400-year time frame that the British were in India – from the arrival of the East India Company (EIC) in the port of Surat, Gujarat in 1608 to the end of the British Raj in 1947 – their palates changed dramatically. From fully embracing everything that India had to offer when it came to spice-laden dishes, to bastardising classic recipes with a more British spin, over time these tweaks and twists resulted in recipes that looked and tasted nothing like the original. Many of those new recipes found themselves back on British shores, with the original source disappearing from public consciousness. Looking even further back in time, the term 'curry' did not exist before Europeans set foot in India. Dishes were described by the specific protein, vegetable or fruit that was being prepared. It was the Portuguese who first coined the word, although they spelt it *caril* or *caree*, to describe the 'broths' which the Indians 'made with Butter, the Pulp of Indian Nuts… and all sorts of Spices, particularly Cardamoms and Ginger…besides herbs, fruits and a thousand other condiments [which they]…poured in good quantity upon… boyl'd Rice' (*The Travels of Pietro Della Valle in India*, Volume II).

At the time of the EIC, the British who settled in India became known as nabobs. It was this group, consisting mainly of men, who fully embraced all that India had to offer, culinary and otherwise. They 'smoked hookahs, lazed about in cool white linen, and kept Indian mistresses in the purdah quarters of their bungalow' (Lizzie Collingham, *Curry*). After the EIC was abolished, a new breed of gentleman arrived: 'British officers that, defeated by the American rebels, recycled themselves as officers for the Company, and had to prove their worth and their mettle' (William Dalrymple, *White Mughals*). In addition, the memsahibs – British ladies – arrived from Victorian Britain and were eager to instil their stiff attitudes throughout all aspects of life in India. Formal attire was worn each evening, even during the sweltering summers, and traditional English fare was served at mealtimes, including unappetisingly named dishes such as 'mock turtle soup' (which was in fact half a calf's head with the skin on), oyster soup, sheep's tongue glaze, boiled chops with boiled rice and blancmange. There was also a propensity for covering savoury dishes in aspic jelly, which was totally unsuitable for the Indian climate. Curry and rice was not completely abolished, however. It was still served in more casual settings and at breakfast and lunch, as well as in the clubs and officers' mess.

As you will see in this chapter, the British in India (often referred to as Anglo-Indians, along with people of mixed British and Indian heritage) took elements, ingredients and techniques from many different regions of their adopted country and brought them together to create their own new cuisine. 'This homogenisation led to generic pan-Indian cuisines that lost their regionality' (Sejal Sukhadwala, *The Philosophy of Curry*). Many British households in India also had Indian cooks who merged their style of cooking with the demands of their employers, resulting in a fusion of English dishes with Indian sensibilities.

In 2023, I spent some time in Chettinad in the state of Tamil Nadu where I completed a 'master chef' course at The Bangala hotel. I learned about the Nattukottai Chettiars, a community of traders and bankers whose successful exploits took them beyond mainland India to Burma, Ceylon and the Malay Straits. Returning to their homeland, they not only brought great riches to furnish their homes, but also culinary influences that they absorbed into their own cuisine. 'As they became wealthier and more Western-orientated, hobnobbing with the Establishment, they introduced Western cuisine into their homes which was cooked by Goans and others who had worked in European homes and who, in Indian homes, were generally called 'butlers'. Thus emerged 'butler cuisine' – Western fare with an Indian touch' (Sumeet Nair and Meenakashi Meyyappan, *The Bangala Table*). Many of these cooks also worked in the clubs of Madras, Bombay and Calcutta, serving their British clientele who preferred the influence of spice but not the same level of heat as traditional Chettiar food. The dishes typically thought of as examples of butler cuisine are the same, or very similar to, Anglo-Indian cuisine: mulligatawny, soups, mutton chops, cutlets and fritters – all of which you'll find my recipes for in the following pages.

Railway Lamb Curry

Preparation time: 15 minutes

Cooking time: 1 hour 20 minutes (or 25 minutes in pressure cooker, see notes on page 9)

Serves 4-6

For the masala

1 tbsp coriander seeds

1 tbsp cumin seeds

1 tbsp fennel seeds

8 black peppercorns

2 dried whole red chillies

For the sauce

30g tamarind pulp or 2 tsp tamarind paste or 1 tsp tamarind concentrate

3 tbsp vegetable, sunflower or rapeseed oil

2 large white onions, finely chopped

1 tsp fine salt

1 stem of fresh or frozen curry leaves (around 15 leaves)

3 green cardamom pods, kept whole but lightly bashed

1 black cardamom pod

4 cloves

3-inch piece of cinnamon or cassia bark

¼ tsp freshly grated nutmeg

2 tsp finely grated fresh ginger

2 tsp finely grated garlic or 4 garlic cloves, finely grated

1 tsp ground turmeric

1 tsp Kashmiri chilli powder

1kg lamb neck or shoulder, cut into bite-size pieces (on or off the bone)

500ml lamb or vegetable stock

2 large potatoes, peeled and chopped into 6 pieces

150ml coconut milk

Luxurious dining carriages were adopted from the mid-nineteenth century in India, serving a fusion of British and Indian delights to appeal to their guests. The 'railway curry' used mutton (often used to describe goat in India) which I've replaced with lamb. It became so popular that all the grandest hotels across India included it on their menus. How it came into existence is a little hazy, but it is thought that it was created for a British officer who visited the onboard kitchen when feeling peckish on a long train journey. The staff were eating a Calcutta *mangsho jhol*, a mutton curry with potatoes and mustard oil. In order to tone down its heat, they added coconut milk (some sources say yoghurt too) and the officer was so blown away by this creation that he ordered it on all his railway journeys thereafter.

1. Begin by dry roasting the spices in a frying pan to make the masala. Move them around the pan for a minute and then place in a spice grinder or pestle and mortar and grind to a fine powder. Set aside for now.

2. If using tamarind pulp, place in a small bowl and cover with warm water. Leave it to soak for 10 minutes then use your whole hand to break it up completely. Strain through a sieve into a bowl and use the back of a spoon to push through all the pulp. Discard the fibrous parts and seeds. Set the pulp aside while you make the curry.

3. Heat the oil in a large pan (I like to use cast iron) and when hot, but on a low heat, add the onion and salt and allow to lightly bronze over the next 8 to 10 minutes.

4. Stir the fresh curry leaves, cardamom pods, cloves, cinnamon or cassia bark and grated nutmeg into the onions.

5. Add the ginger and garlic, then leave to cook gently for the next 3 minutes, which will take away their rawness.

6. Add the ground spice masala you prepared earlier, along with the ground turmeric and Kashmiri chilli powder. Mix all the spices in well before adding the lamb pieces.

7. Add the stock to the pan and simmer gently for 40 minutes. At this stage, you can cook it on the hob or transfer the pan to a preheated oven at 200°C/180°C fan/400°F/Gas 6.

8. Add the potatoes to the pan and cook for 15 to 20 minutes until softened. Remove the pan from the oven or take it off the heat.

9. Add the tamarind pulp, paste or concentrate and the coconut milk to the curry. (If you add the coconut milk while the pan is on the heat, it will split). Stir in well and then return to the hob and heat to just below boiling point.

10. Simmer until the gravy has thickened to your liking and the meat has softened sufficiently. If you remove the lid from the pan and keep it on a low heat, it will thicken up nicely. Check the seasoning and add more salt as required before serving.

Notes: Instead of using large potatoes you can add 10 to 12 new potatoes, left whole with their skins on, in Step 8. I like to use Kashmiri chilli powder as it provides colour and very little heat. Deggi Mirch is another option, which contains Kashmiri chilli and red bell peppers. If you use a generic chilli powder, use a little less than suggested in the recipe as it will likely be hotter.

Chicken Korma

Preparation time: 10 minutes
Cooking time: 50 minutes
Serves 4-6

6 tbsp vegetable, sunflower or rapeseed oil

4 large white onions, finely sliced

1½ tsp fine salt

2 Indian bay leaves (or European bay leaves)

2 x 2-inch pieces of cinnamon or cassia bark

4-6 dried whole red chillies

6 cloves

8 green cardamom pods, opened

2 large white onions, finely chopped

2 tsp finely grated fresh ginger

1 tsp finely grated garlic

1kg chicken thighs, skinned and cut into bite-size pieces (or on the bone: see notes)

2 tsp ground coriander

150g natural yoghurt

150ml water

1 lime, juiced

The origin of the 'khoormah', 'quormah' or korma as it is more often to referred to in the British Isles is an Islamic dish that came to India via the Mughals of central Asia. The British, from the time of the East India Company and later the British Raj, enjoyed their chicken and lamb kormas immensely and, as the wife of a retired Indian officer wrote in 1895, 'if made successfully, constituted an agreeable change from English curries'. Recipes for a korma were included in most of the cookery books printed in India for a British readership during the nineteenth and twentieth centuries. Almonds and rose essence were not listed as ingredients, where they often would be in recipes today, but lemongrass and lime were sometimes suggested. Interestingly, tomatoes were not used in korma at that time, unlike some contemporary recipes. This recipe is inspired by C. C. Kohlhoff's 'quoormah curry' from the book *Indian Cookery and Domestic Recipes* which was published in Madras in 1906. It's quite different from the kormas at curry houses across the UK, but I hope will be even more agreeable to your palate. Give it a whirl!

1. Heat 4 tablespoons of the oil in a deep, heavy-based pan and when hot, lower the heat. Add the 4 sliced white onions with half a teaspoon of the salt to help them release water.

2. Allow the onions to brown for 20 minutes. Remove the onions from the pan and once cooled, blitz in a blender until smooth. Set aside.

3. Using the same pan, heat the remaining oil and then add the bay leaves, cinnamon or cassia bark, dried red chillies, cloves, green cardamom, and the 2 chopped white onions. Move everything around the pan on a low heat for 8 minutes before adding the grated ginger and garlic.

4. After a further 3 to 4 minutes, add the chicken thighs and stir to coat them in the spices and onions. Add the ground coriander, remaining teaspoon of salt and the blended onions you prepared earlier, mixing well.

5. Lower the heat, add the yoghurt and water and simmer gently for 30 to 40 minutes, adding a little more water if it becomes too dry. At this stage, you can transfer the korma to a preheated oven at 200°C/180°C fan/400°F/Gas 6 or continue to cook on the hob.

6. Before serving, add the lime juice and taste to check the seasoning. Enjoy with some steamed basmati rice or Parsi 'Brown' Rice (page 186) to mop up the juices.

Notes: You can make this curry with chicken thighs on the bone if you prefer; they will just need a little longer to cook than chicken off the bone and you will need about 1.3kg in total – ask your butcher to skin and chop the chicken into bite-size pieces. Either way, don't discard the chicken skin! Instead, spread it out on greaseproof paper, sprinkle with a little sea salt and black pepper and place in a hot oven for around 15 minutes or until crispy. These crispy skins make a great snack or side to have alongside your chicken korma.

Country Captain Chicken

Preparation time: 10 minutes
Cooking time: 30-40 minutes
Serves 4

2 tbsp vegetable oil or ghee (clarified butter)

3 large onions, finely sliced

1 tsp fine salt

4 cloves

2-inch piece of cinnamon or cassia bark

2 tsp finely grated fresh ginger

4 garlic cloves, roughly chopped

2-3 fresh green or red chillies, finely diced

800g chicken thighs, skinned and cut into bite-size pieces (or on the bone with skin)

2 tsp freshly ground black pepper

1 tsp ground turmeric

200ml chicken stock

Juice of ½ a lemon

'Country Captain' was one of the most well-known dishes during the Raj. 'Country' refers to India as opposed to Britain, and according to David Burton in his book *A Raj at the Table*, its origin could have been a reference to the captain in charge of *sepoys* – Indian soldiers within the European military. It could also have been a reference to a naval captain, as the recipe made its way to English ports as well as the American South. It's very straightforward to prepare with only a few ingredients required, which may explain its popularity. I think it makes the perfect midweek meal.

1. Heat the oil or ghee in a large pan and add the sliced onions. Add the salt and allow the onions to bronze gently over the next 6 to 8 minutes.

2. Remove a tablespoonful of the onions, place in a small dish and set aside.

3. Add the cloves, cinnamon or cassia bark, ginger, garlic and fresh chillies to the remaining onions in the pan and mix well.

4. After a couple of minutes, add the chicken (if you are using chicken thighs on the bone, place them into the pan skin-side down), black pepper and ground turmeric.

5. Give everything a stir, add the stock and allow to simmer gently for 20 to 30 minutes. Chicken on the bone will take a little longer, around 30 to 40 minutes. At this stage, you can transfer the pan to a preheated oven at 200°C/180°C fan/400°F/Gas 6 if you prefer. If it looks dry, just add a little water.

6. Once the chicken is cooked through, add the lemon juice and taste to check the seasoning.

7. Finally, in your smallest saucepan, heat enough oil to coat the bottom of the pan by approximately half an inch (1-2cm). When hot, add the tablespoonful of onion you set aside earlier and allow it to crisp up over the next 3 to 4 minutes. Remove with a slotted spoon and place on some kitchen paper to drain the excess oil.

8. Scatter the crispy onions over the dish and enjoy.

Notes: If you'd like the dish to have less heat, slice the chillies in half lengthways instead of finely dicing them, adding at the same point during cooking.

Frithath Beef Curry

Preparation time: 15-20 minutes
Cooking time: 1 hour 45 minutes (or
40 minutes in pressure cooker, see
notes on page 9)
Serves 4-6

For the dry roast masala

10 black peppercorns

6 dried whole red chillies

5 green cardamom pods

4 cloves

2-inch piece of cinnamon or cassia bark

1 tsp cumin seeds

1 tbsp white or cider vinegar

For the sauce

1 tbsp ghee or 2 tbsp vegetable,
sunflower or rapeseed oil

4 fresh green chillies, split lengthways

2 large onions, sliced

1 tsp fine salt

30g tamarind pulp or 2 tsp tamarind
paste or 1 tsp tamarind concentrate

2 heaped tsp finely grated fresh ginger

10 garlic cloves, kept whole

1kg chuck or braising beef, cut into
bite-size cubes

1 tsp ground turmeric

400ml water

'This is a very hot curry, too hot for most people' was the verdict of Navroji Framji in *Indian Cookery for Young Housekeepers*, published in 1887. That piqued my interest in this recipe and the version here is loosely based on the original in that book. Frithath, also known as *fritthad*, originates from Eastern India and is a ground, wet masala that is dry roasted to begin with.

1. Preheat your oven to 200°C/180°C fan/400°F/Gas 6.

2. First, dry roast all the masala spices in a saucepan without any oil. Move them around the pan for 1 to 2 minutes, allowing them to release their aromas. Remove them from the heat and leave to cool before grinding in a spice grinder or pestle and mortar to form a fine powder. Place in a bowl and stir in the vinegar to form a wet paste.

3. In a pan, heat the ghee or oil and then add the green chillies, sliced onion and salt. On a low heat, allow this to soften and lightly bronze for around 8 minutes.

4. Meanwhile, if using tamarind pulp, place the pulp in a small bowl and cover with warm water. Leave it to soak for 10 minutes then use your whole hand to break it up completely. Strain through a sieve into a bowl and use the back of a spoon to push through all the pulp. Discard the fibrous parts and seeds.

5. Add the grated ginger and garlic cloves to the pan of chillies and onions. Stir well, then after a couple of minutes, add the beef. Stir well and allow the cubes to brown on all sides over a low heat, adding a little more ghee or oil as required.

6. Add the masala paste and ground turmeric to the pan, followed by the prepared tamarind pulp, paste or concentrate and 400ml of water.

7. Allow the beef to cook slowly over a low heat for 1 hour 30 minutes. Taste before serving to check the seasoning, adding more salt if required and/or a little sugar to balance out any sourness from the tamarind. The beef should be beautifully tender when done.

Notes: Tamarind pulp, as opposed to paste or concentrate, is available at Asian grocery stores and some large supermarkets, usually found in block form wrapped in cellophane. It stores in the fridge for months. I tend to buy it in this form but tamarind paste is equally good. If you buy tamarind concentrate, use with caution as it's much stronger in flavour.

Fruity Meat Glassy

Preparation time: 10 minutes
Cooking time: 1 hour 40 minutes
Serves 4-6

2-3 tbsp vegetable, sunflower or rapeseed oil

2 large white onions, finely chopped

1 tsp fine salt

2 tsp finely grated garlic

2 tsp finely grated fresh ginger

½ tsp freshly ground black pepper

1-2 tsp Kashmiri chilli powder

4 large tomatoes, finely chopped or 200ml tinned tomatoes

800g beef chuck or stewing steak

350ml water

2 medium potatoes, peeled and quartered

2 tbsp white or cider vinegar

2 tsp sugar

1 tbsp sweet mango chutney (optional, see recipe on page 82)

The name of this much-loved Anglo-Indian recipe derives from the tomato-based glaze that coats the meat. Beef was commonly used, but you could also use lamb, pork or goat. A little vinegar and sugar give it sweet and sour notes and some recipes recommend stirring in a dollop of sweet mango chutney just before serving.

1. Heat the oil in a large cast iron pot or casserole. On a medium to low heat, add the onions and salt. Allow the onions to bronze for around 10 minutes, stirring intermittently to avoid them catching on the bottom of the pan.

2. Once the onions have nicely bronzed, add the grated garlic and ginger along with the freshly ground black pepper and Kashmiri chilli powder. Keep everything moving around the pan for 4 minutes, then add the fresh or tinned tomatoes.

3. Allow the tomatoes to cook down and wait for the oil to separate, which will take around 6 minutes. Now add the beef and coat in the spiced masala. Allow the beef to begin to bronze over the next 8 to 10 minutes.

4. Add the water to the pot, cover with a lid and stir intermittently over the next 40 minutes. At this stage, you can move the pot to a preheated oven at 180°C/160°C fan/350°F/Gas 4 rather than cooking on the hob, checking at intervals that it has enough water.

5. After 40 minutes add the potatoes, vinegar and sugar with enough water to cover the potatoes. Return to the hob or oven for a further 25 minutes.

6. Once cooked, allow the dish to rest for 10 minutes before serving. Check the seasoning and then add the sweet mango chutney if using, stirring it into the gravy just before serving. Enjoy with some steamed basmati rice.

Notes: If you want to make the dish vegetarian, I suggest using squash, pumpkin or jackfruit instead of the beef and reducing the cooking time by half. In India, this dish is usually made in a pressure cooker, but I use my cast iron pot. If you have a pressure cooker it will take around 30 minutes, but the oven method will taste equally good, it just takes longer for the meat to soften and the flavours to infuse.

Kedgeree

Preparation time: 10 minutes
Cooking time: 12 minutes
Serves 4

400ml milk or water

2 European bay leaves

4 black peppercorns

2 cloves

400g smoked haddock

4 eggs

200g long grain basmati rice

80g unsalted butter

1 heaped tsp mild curry powder (or Madras curry powder, see page 80)

Salt and pepper, to taste

Handful of fresh parsley, finely chopped

1 lemon, quartered

Drizzle of single cream, to serve (optional)

This dish started life as *khichiri*, a comforting ayurvedic breakfast dish consisting of rice, lentils and spices, which is still popular in India today. The British in India began by eating it this way, but over time a 'hybrid emerged out of the relationship between Indian cooks and the wives of Company officials. In the belief that dining remained an essential component of British identity, the latter generally insisted on adapting the recipe to their own culinary tastes' as Ishita Banerjee-Dube describes in her essay 'Modern Mixes: The Hybrid and the Authentic in Indian Cuisine'. Lentils were removed and flaked fish was added along with boiled egg. Back in Britain, the name changed to kedgeree and one of its earliest recipes was written around 1790 in the cookery book of a Scottish housewife, Stephana Malcolm, whose brothers had spent time in India. Items that were hard to source, such as curry leaves, were substituted – namely with cayenne pepper in this case – and curry powder became a staple, pushing aside whole spices. Today, kedgeree continues to be loved in both Britain and India with everyone putting their own spin on it.

1.   Begin by gently heating the milk or water on a low heat along with the bay leaves, peppercorns and cloves.

2.   Add the smoked haddock to this infusion and continue to heat through for 10 minutes. Remove the haddock from the pan with a slotted spoon and discard the cooking liquor. Remove the skin from the haddock and discard. Gently break up the flesh and set aside.

3.   Bring a small pan of water to the boil, gently lower the eggs into the water and cook for 8 minutes until hard-boiled. Remove from the pan and submerge in cold water before carefully removing the shells, then roughly chop the hard-boiled eggs and set aside.

4.   Wash the rice gently with cold water, being careful not to break the grains, then drain and transfer to a pan. Cover with cold water so that it sits an inch above the rice. Bring to the boil, then turn the heat down and simmer gently, uncovered, for 10 minutes. Check at around 8 minutes that it is almost soft and not overcooking. Once the grains have lost their bite, drain the rice and briefly run it under cold water to stop it cooking further.

5.   Melt the butter in a wide, deep pan and then add the curry powder followed by the smoked haddock and cooked rice. Gently fold everything together, seasoning with salt and pepper if required.

6.   Add the chopped egg and then serve the kedgeree with a scattering of chopped parsley and lemon wedges on top. If you fancy, finish with a drizzle of single cream for added decadence.

Notes: While kedgeree is traditionally regarded as a breakfast meal, it's equally delicious for lunch or supper. If you are preparing this for more than 4 people, add an extra egg and 50g more rice per person.

Mulligatawny

Preparation time: 15 minutes
Cooking time: 20 minutes
Serves 6

2 tbsp vegetable oil

1 onion, roughly chopped

2 celery sticks, roughly chopped

2 carrots, roughly chopped

1 apple, cored and roughly chopped

3 garlic cloves, roughly chopped

1-inch piece (15g) of fresh ginger, thinly sliced

200g boneless chicken thighs, roughly chopped

50g red split lentils

2 heaped tsp Madras curry powder (see page 80), garam masala or store-bought curry powder

1 tsp freshly ground black pepper

½ tsp ground turmeric

1.5 litres chicken stock

1 tsp salt, or to taste

Juice of ½ a lemon

Perhaps the most well known and loved of all Anglo-Indian dishes is mulligatawny, which derives from the South Indian *rasam*, a spiced broth. The name translates simply as 'pepper water' in Tamil. It combined the British love of soups with just a hint of Indian spice in the form of a Madras curry powder, along with vegetables and sometimes meat too. It was on the menu at all the clubs and British officers even 'carried it in flasks on expeditions in the hills as fortification against the cold' according to David Burton's *A Raj at the Table*. Mulligatawny is a versatile soup that can include meat or be made completely vegetarian. Traditionally, it's served over a spoonful of cooked rice placed in each bowl.

1. Heat the oil in a deep pan. Add the onion, celery, carrot and apple. Move everything around the pan for 5 minutes before adding the garlic and ginger, followed by the chicken. Mix well to combine everything and cook evenly.

2. After a further 3 to 4 minutes, add the red split lentils, Madras curry powder, black pepper and ground turmeric.

3. Add the chicken stock and then simmer gently for 15 minutes. After this time, check to see if the carrot has softened and then use a stick blender to blitz into a smooth soup. Add more water if you prefer a thinner consistency.

4. Add the salt and taste to check the seasoning before finally stirring in the lemon juice. You can serve the mulligatawny as is, or – to serve it as they often did in India – add a heaped spoonful of cooked rice to each bowl and then ladle the soup on top.

Notes: Try to cut the onion, celery, carrot and apple to roughly the same size so that they cook evenly. If you want to buy a curry powder, opt for mild or medium curry powder or garam masala. You can use leftover chicken or turkey instead of fresh chicken or leave the meat out altogether and use vegetable stock. The finished soup freezes well, so it's a great recipe for making larger batches in advance.

Stuffed Aubergine Cutlets

Preparation time: 20 minutes
Cooking time: 40 minutes
Serves 6

3 medium or large aubergines

2 tbsp vegetable, sunflower or rapeseed oil

1 large or 2 medium white onions, finely diced

1 tsp fine salt

2 garlic cloves, finely grated

1 tsp finely grated fresh ginger

2 large tomatoes, finely diced

500g chicken mince

Large handful of fresh mint, finely chopped

2 fresh green chillies, finely chopped

½ tsp freshly ground black pepper

½ tsp ground turmeric

2 eggs, beaten

Handful of fine breadcrumbs (not panko)

Aubergines, or eggplants as they are also known, are wonderful vehicles for stuffing. The British loved cutlets of all kinds (see page 74 for a prawn version) and for this dish you can use any meat or non-meat mince as part of the stuffing. Typically, it was made with beef mince, but I like to make it with chicken – though you could also use pork, lamb, tofu or paneer. This recipe is adapted from the late Copeland Marks who lived in India for some years and wrote the book *The Varied Kitchens of India*.

1. Begin by bringing a pan of water to the boil. Cut the aubergines in half lengthways, then submerge them in the boiling water for 5 minutes. Remove and drain on kitchen paper.

2. Scoop out and finely dice the aubergine flesh, leaving half an inch attached to the skin so the aubergine holds its shape.

3. Heat the oil in a large frying pan and when hot, add the onion and salt. Allow to lightly bronze over the next 6 to 8 minutes.

4. Add the garlic and ginger to the pan, mix well and cook with the onion for the following 3 minutes. Now add the diced tomatoes and cook for another couple of minutes until softened and broken down. Meanwhile, preheat the oven to 200°C/180°C fan/400°F/Gas 6.

5. Add the diced aubergine, chicken mince, fresh mint, chillies, black pepper and ground turmeric to the pan with a little more oil if necessary. Once the mince has changed colour after 5 minutes, mix well until everything is combined. Taste to check the seasoning and add more salt as required.

6. Using a large spoon, stuff the aubergine shells with the mince mixture, filling them right to the top. Spoon over some beaten egg and then sprinkle breadcrumbs over each stuffed aubergine.

7. Place the stuffed aubergines on an ovenproof tray and bake in the preheated oven for 15 minutes. Once cooked, pop them under the grill for another 3 minutes to lightly char the tops, then serve warm.

Country Captain Vegetables

Preparation time: 10 minutes
Cooking time: 20 minutes
Serves 4-6

The vegetarian version of 'Country Captain' evolved after the chicken version and doesn't use any whole spices, instead using a ground spice blend. My Madras curry powder works really well here. Once the prep is done, the dish itself takes no time to cook.

250g potatoes, diced

250g carrots, diced

250g frozen or fresh peas

250g frozen or fresh green or runner beans, finely diced

20g tamarind pulp or 2 tsp tamarind paste or 1 tsp tamarind concentrate

2 tbsp vegetable, sunflower or rapeseed oil

6 spring onions, sliced

4 garlic cloves, roughly chopped

2 tsp Madras curry powder (store-bought or see recipe on page 80)

1 tsp fine salt, or to taste

50g freshly grated or desiccated coconut

1.   Bring a pan of water to the boil and then add the potatoes and carrots, as they take a little longer to soften.

2.   After 6 minutes, add the peas and beans. Simmer for a further 6 to 8 minutes or until the vegetables have softened. Check they are all tender before draining and setting aside.

3.   While the vegetables are boiling, if using tamarind pulp, place the pulp in a small bowl and cover with warm water. Leave it to soak for 10 minutes then use your whole hand to break it up completely. Strain through a sieve into a bowl and use the back of a spoon to push through all the pulp. Discard the fibrous parts and seeds.

4.   In a wide pan, heat the oil and add the spring onions and garlic. Stir in the Madras curry powder and then add the prepared tamarind pulp, paste or concentrate. If using tamarind paste or concentrate, add 50ml of water at the same time. Mix well before adding the drained vegetables. Gently stir all the ingredients together.

5.   Add the salt and simmer for 5 minutes. Check that all the vegetables have softened to a nice texture, then add the grated or desiccated coconut, mix well and serve.

Notes: It's important to dice the potatoes, carrots and green or runner beans evenly so they all cook in the same amount of time. Frozen beans, peas and carrots are also great for this recipe and taste equally good. For the freshly grated coconut, I tend to make a batch and store the rest in the freezer, as it can be used straight from frozen. Alternatively, you can buy frozen grated coconut, or desiccated coconut also works really well.

Courgette and Prawn Foogath

Preparation time: 10 minutes
Cooking time: 15 minutes
Serves 4

3 tbsp coconut oil

1 tsp black or brown mustard seeds

1 stem of fresh or frozen curry leaves (around 15 leaves)

2-3 fresh or frozen chillies, sliced diagonally

1 large white onion, finely chopped

3 garlic cloves, finely chopped

½ tsp ground turmeric

600g medium prawns, cleaned and deveined

3 courgettes, peeled and sliced into ½ inch half-moons

2 small handfuls of desiccated or freshly grated coconut

1 tsp fine salt, or to taste

The British in India always loved the very simple method of cooking vegetables known as 'foogath' – stir frying them with a little oil, mustard seeds, onions, garlic, chillies and grated coconut. It takes minutes to make and yet elevates the humblest of vegetables. The term is of Mangalorean and Goan origin and is very similar to a Keralan *thoran*, a Tamil Nadu *poriyal* and a Sri Lankan *mallum*. In India, the British would have likely used ridge gourds, which are available at most Asian grocers here in the UK, but you could use any of the following: courgettes, okra, cabbage, asparagus, pumpkin, beetroot, French beans, cabbage or cauliflower. Play around with whichever vegetable takes your fancy. Adding the prawns is a delicious addition, but you can easily leave them out to make this a tasty vegan dish.

1. In a medium pan, heat the coconut oil and then add the mustard seeds. They will begin to splutter so make sure the heat is not too high.

2. Add the curry leaves and chillies followed by the onion. Simmer gently in the pan for 3 minutes before adding the garlic. You want the onion and garlic to soften but not brown, so keep moving them around the pan for a further minute.

3. Add the turmeric followed by the prawns. Stir well for a couple of minutes so that they are thoroughly coated in the spices and then add the courgettes and salt. Lower the heat and place a lid on the pan.

4. Every few minutes, stir the foogath and then replace the lid, allowing the mixture to steam in the water released from the prawns and courgettes.

5. After 8 to 10 minutes, everything should be cooked through. Taste to check the seasoning and then scatter the desiccated or freshly grated coconut into the pan.

6. Gently fold the coconut into the foogath, then serve immediately.

Notes: If you can find ridge gourds (also known as *toriya* or *turia*) you can replace the courgettes with them, although you will probably need only two, depending on their size. Peel them as you would a courgette. If you are using frozen prawns, remove them from the freezer and run them under cold water in a colander, then place them in a large bowl of cold water for 10 minutes before rinsing again under cold water. Do not run warm or hot water over them.

Pumpkin and Tamarind Soup

Preparation time: 15 minutes
Cooking time: 35 minutes
Serves 4

2 tbsp vegetable, sunflower or rapeseed oil

2 white onions, roughly chopped

1 tsp fine salt

2 garlic cloves, roughly chopped

1 heaped tsp roughly chopped ginger

½ tsp dried chilli flakes, plus a little extra to serve

½ tsp ground turmeric

500g pumpkin, peeled, deseeded and cubed

800ml water

1 vegetable stock cube

20g tamarind pulp or 2 tsp tamarind paste or 1 tsp tamarind concentrate

1 tsp fine brown or caster sugar

100ml coconut milk

Soups, or *shorbas* as they are often referred to in India, have always been popular with the British. Having a soup as an actual course or indeed a meal in itself is as common now as it was for the British in India. In the UK there is always a huge glut of pumpkins and squash in the autumn, so try this soup when you are pondering what to do with them all. It freezes well too.

1. Heat the oil in a pan, add the onions and salt and allow to soften and very lightly bronze over the next 5 minutes.

2. Stir the garlic, ginger and dried chilli flakes into the onions. After a couple of minutes, add the turmeric, cubed pumpkin, water and stock cube.

3. Simmer gently for 15 minutes, ensuring the pumpkin is covered with the water, or until the pumpkin is completely soft.

4. If using tamarind pulp, place in a small bowl and cover with warm water. Leave it to soak for 10 minutes then use your whole hand to break it up completely. Strain through a sieve into a bowl and use the back of a spoon to push through all the pulp. Discard the fibrous parts and seeds.

5. Add the tamarind pulp, paste or concentrate to the pan along with the sugar and then use a handheld blender to blend until smooth.

6. Simmer the soup gently on a low heat and then add the coconut milk. Taste to check the balance of sweet, sour and salty flavours, then serve with extra dried chilli flakes on top.

Notes: You can replace the pumpkin with butternut squash if you prefer. Tamarind pulp, as opposed to paste or concentrate, is available at Asian grocery stores and some large supermarkets, usually found in block form wrapped in cellophane. It stores in the fridge for months. I tend to buy it in this form but tamarind paste is equally good. If you buy tamarind concentrate, use with caution as it's much stronger in flavour.

Prawn Cutlets

Preparation time: 30-40 minutes
Cooking time: 15 minutes
Makes 14

1kg shell-on prawns or 550g prawns without shells

2 slices of white bread

1 onion, finely chopped

1-2 fresh green chillies, finely chopped

3 garlic cloves, finely grated or 1 heaped tsp garlic paste

2 tsp finely grated fresh ginger or ginger paste

1 egg, whisked

Handful of fresh mint leaves, finely chopped

¼ tsp ground turmeric

1 tsp salt

½ tsp freshly ground black pepper

6 tbsp panko breadcrumbs

6 tbsp vegetable, sunflower or rapeseed oil

Cutlets of all varieties – in this context meaning pounded meat, fish or prawns made into a breadcrumbed patty and lightly fried – were hugely popular in British India. They can be found in many recipe books from nineteenth-century India and are as irresistibly moreish now as they were then. The addition of fresh mint, as opposed to coriander, gives them a British twist since mint has been used in British cuisine for centuries, dating back to medieval times. The Victorians were particularly fond of fresh mint, which thrived in our temperate climate, and the prominence of fresh coriander in Asian dishes has risen more recently due to the UK's openness to global flavours. Eaten alongside a chutney, these cutlets make a very tasty snack.

1. First, remove the shells from the prawns. Place the shells and heads in a sealable bag and store in your freezer; they are great to have on hand for making prawn bisques.

2. Devein and clean the prawns, then finely chop them and place in a mixing bowl.

3. Soak the white bread briefly in water, then squeeze out the water and break up the soaked bread with your hands. Add this to the mixing bowl.

4. Add all the remaining ingredients except the breadcrumbs and oil to the mixing bowl. Pour the panko breadcrumbs into a separate shallow bowl.

5. Use your hands to form a small patty with the prawn mixture, about 2 inches (5cm) in diameter, and flatten slightly with the palm of your hand. Repeat with all the mixture.

6. Pour half the oil into a frying pan on a low heat. While it warms up, coat the prawn patties in the panko breadcrumbs and then lower them carefully into the frying pan. Cook the patties in batches so as not to overcrowd the pan.

7. Keep the oil on a low heat and lightly bronze the patties all over. This should take around 2 to 3 minutes per side.

8. Once cooked, remove the patties from the pan and place on kitchen paper to drain. Serve them with the Himalayan Hot Sauce on page 176 or my Mango Chutney (see page 82). I also like to serve these alongside Allegra's Kachumber Salad on page 76.

Allegra's Kachumber Salad

Preparation time: 15 minutes
Makes a large bowlful

1 red onion, thinly sliced
2 large cucumbers, roughly chopped
8 medium tomatoes, roughly diced
Handful of fresh coriander, chopped
1-2 tsp freshly ground black pepper
Fine salt, to taste
1-2 limes, juiced
Drizzle of olive oil

Kachumber salad is the most ubiquitous salad in the whole of India and balances out many curries with some crunch, a little heat and clean flavours. It's quick to rustle up and works so well with many of the curries in this book, which is why I've included it here. There is a version of kachumber salad in my first cookbook, *Chilli & Mint: Indian Home Cooking from a British Kitchen*, but this one has been adapted by my daughter Allegra and uses no chilli, only freshly ground black pepper. The British in India would undoubtedly have loved it, and it's now well-known across the whole of the Indian subcontinent.

1. Place all the ingredients except the lime juice and olive oil in a large bowl. Mix well.
2. Add the juice of 1 lime and the olive oil to the bowl, then use salad servers to toss the salad, coating it in this light dressing. Add extra lime juice to taste.
3. This salad is best served immediately once the dressing has been added.

Pish Pash

Preparation time: 10 minutes
Cooking time: 30 minutes for brown
rice or 20 minutes for white rice
Serves 4

2 tbsp vegetable, sunflower or
rapeseed oil

2 x 2-inch pieces of cinnamon or cassia
bark

2 black cardamom pods

5 cloves

1 tsp black peppercorns, roughly
crushed in a pestle and mortar

1 onion, finely sliced into half moons

1 tsp finely grated garlic

2-inch piece (30g) of fresh ginger,
peeled and cut into fine batons

1 tsp salt, or to taste

250g chicken thighs, cut into small bite-
size pieces

150g white or brown basmati rice

1 lemon, juice only

1 litre chicken or vegetable stock

Freshly ground black pepper, to taste

1 tbsp ghee or butter, to serve
(optional)

Fresh mint or coriander, finely chopped
(optional)

A favourite of the British in colonial India was a dish affectionately known as 'pish pash'. It is thought that the name derives from the Persian 'push-pash' which means 'bits and bobs' and fittingly describes the dish's medley of textures. This one-pot meal comprised meat (often chicken) and rice with a few whole spices thrown in, plus onion, garlic and ginger and occasionally potatoes too. The British loved nursery-style comfort food and this dish ticked all those boxes. It would have been given to those who were feeling under the weather and to children because it's easy to digest. Similar to a *congee* or *khichiri* in consistency, it's the perfect dish to make if you have a propensity to overcook your rice, which is actually encouraged in this recipe.

1. Begin by heating the oil and when hot, add the cinnamon or cassia bark, black cardamon, cloves and crushed black peppercorns, followed by the onion.

2. Keep everything moving around the pan for 3 minutes before adding the garlic, fresh ginger batons and salt.

3. Add the chicken and stir to coat all the pieces in the spices and onions. After a couple of minutes add the basmati rice, lemon juice and chicken or vegetable stock.

4. Bring to the boil and then cover with a lid. Stir intermittently and add a little hot water as required. Cook for 30 minutes if using brown basmati rice and 20 minutes if using white. This should be a soupy rice dish, slightly wetter than a risotto.

5. Once the rice looks as if it has overcooked and has a sticky quality, the dish is ready. Season with black pepper and, if using, stir in the ghee or butter, then scatter with fresh coriander or mint. Serve with some chutney on the side.

Notes: To make this vegetarian, simply substitute the chicken with either red split (*masoor*) lentils or yellow moong/mung lentils. Sometimes I like to add a couple of cubed potatoes too.

Madras Curry Powder

Preparation time: 5 minutes
Cooking time: 5 minutes
Makes 1 small jar

2 tbsp coriander seeds

1 tbsp cumin seeds

1 tsp fennel seeds

1 tsp fenugreek seeds

1 tsp black peppercorns

5 cloves

8 green cardamom pods

2-inch piece of cinnamon or cassia bark

2-4 dried whole red chillies (use Kashmiri chillies if you want less heat)

15 fresh curry leaves (optional, but recommended)

1 tsp ground turmeric

The mild, medium and hot curry powders that are the mainstays of so many western spice racks are in fact a British invention. In India, masalas, which are a blend of spices, were typically made fresh and would vary depending on the recipe, the most common and well known being garam masala. It was the British who created the generic mild, medium and hot curry powders along with the Madras, which was thought of as slightly hotter than a general curry powder. Those returning to Britain adored these curry powders, as they reminded them of India and the flavours they craved. In powdered form, it was easy to transport and add to any meal for a generic hint of exotic spices.

1. Heat a large frying pan and first add all the seeds, black peppercorns, cloves, cardamom pods, cinnamon or cassia bark and chillies. Move them around the pan for a minute before adding the fresh curry leaves, if using.

2. Continue to gently move the spices around the pan for a further minute. This releases all their natural oils and will bring a great aroma to the masala.

3. Pour the spices into a bowl and leave to cool. Blitz all the ingredients in a spice grinder, along with the ground turmeric, to make your Madras curry powder.

4. Store in an airtight jar and use within 3 months.

Notes: If you can't get dried whole chillies, you can add chilli powder to taste instead. Madras curry powder is made very much according to personal taste so play around with the spices to suit your palate – but coriander, cumin, turmeric, cinnamon and fenugreek seeds are a must.

Mango Chutney

Preparation time: 20 minutes
Cooking time: 25 minutes
Makes 3 jam jars

2 tbsp vegetable oil

2-inch piece of cinnamon or cassia bark, broken in half

7 green cardamom pods, husks removed and discarded

4 cloves, crushed

2 tsp nigella seeds

1 tsp cumin seeds

½ tsp ground turmeric

1 tsp chilli flakes (optional)

½ tsp Kashmiri chilli powder

3 large mangoes (approx. 1kg), finely diced

4 garlic cloves, finely diced or 2 tsp grated garlic

2 tsp finely grated fresh ginger or 1 tsp ground ginger

150g caster or fine brown sugar

200ml white wine or cider vinegar

100ml water

1 tsp salt

2 tsp cornflour

3 tbsp cold water

The British in India adored the sweet, sour and tangy chutneys served at mealtimes, with mango chutney being a firm favourite. Typically, chutneys – unlike pickles or achar as they are known in India – were served fresh and consumed immediately as they did not contain vinegar and would spoil quickly in the heat. The British version of mango chutney did include vinegar, allowing preservation for many months in sterilised jars, which was perfect for long voyages overseas. The chutney became so popular that it was rolled out whenever curry was on the menu and even today in Britain, most curry house meals will begin with mango chutney and poppadums.

1. Heat the oil in a medium pan on a low heat. Add all the whole spices and move them around the pan for 10 to 20 seconds.

2. Add the ground turmeric, chilli flakes and Kashmiri chilli powder to the pan immediately followed by the mango, garlic and ginger. Mix well.

3. Stir in the sugar, vinegar, water and salt and simmer gently for 25 minutes. Taste to check the seasoning, then add more salt, sugar or chilli flakes as required. If it needs thickening, combine the cornflour and cold water in a small bowl and then stir into the chutney.

4. Transfer the chutney to sterilised jars and store in a cool place until ready to consume. Unopened, they will last for up to 6 months. Once opened, consume within 2 weeks and store in the fridge.

Syrian Christian

One of the oldest Christian communities in the world can be found in the southwestern state of Kerala. Known as Syrian Christians or Saint Thomas Christians, their ancestry dates back to the very first Indians who were converted to Christianity by Thomas the Apostle, who is believed to have arrived on the Malabar Coast in AD 52. Many of these early converters were Namboodiri Brahmin families, said to have witnessed a miracle by Saint Thomas which involved levitating water and subsequently became committed followers. The name Syrian Christians derives from their liturgy, which was spoken by Jesus and known as Aramaic (Syriac) language. Today these Christians are also known as Nazaranis (the followers of Jesus of Nazareth) and are divided into four sects that all share common religious and social practices.

Their cuisine fuses Hindu cooking practices with influences from Malay, Dutch, Portuguese, Syrian, Chinese and Arab cuisines – brought by traders who were all drawn to Kerala in search of spices – and is a melting pot of flavours and techniques. The abundance of coconut palms in the area meant that coconuts became a key ingredient in the cuisine, from the milk and oil to the roasted, grated or ground flesh. Tapioca, also known as kappa or cassava, is another characteristic element of Syrian Christian dishes, cooked with both meat and fish as well as on its own in a dish called *kappa puzhukku* which you can find on page 106. Stews, frys, roasts, molees and appam are all typical dishes of this community. Some are wet curries with tasty, lightly spiced gravies such as the chicken stew on page 96 while others are drier dishes such as the beef fry on page 88.

The local diet is largely non-vegetarian and features a wide variety of meat, though pork and duck are often reserved for special occasions such as weddings. Seafood has always been an integral part of their cuisine too of course, owing to Kerala's coastal location, as you will see in the recipes that follow.

Black Chickpea Curry

Preparation time: 10-15 minutes
Cooking time: 18 minutes
Makes 4

2 tbsp coconut oil

½ tsp fennel seeds

I tsp black or brown mustard seeds

I stem of fresh or frozen curry leaves
(about 15 leaves)

I medium red onion, thinly sliced

I tsp fine salt

I tsp finely grated garlic

I tsp finely grated fresh ginger

2 tsp ground coriander

I tsp Kashmiri chilli powder

½ tsp ground turmeric

½ tsp freshly ground black pepper

3 medium tomatoes, chopped

2 x 400g black chickpeas or carlin peas
(see above)

I x 400ml tin of coconut milk

150ml water

For the tempering

I tsp coconut oil

½ tsp black or brown mustard seeds

I stem of fresh or frozen curry leaves
(about 15 leaves)

I dried whole red chilli, broken in half

This recipe is known as *kadala kari* in Malayalam, the national language of Kerala. Traditionally it's made with dried black chickpeas that are soaked overnight before boiling in a pressure cooker until soft. For a time-efficient alternative, I suggest either purchasing tinned black chickpeas which are easily available from Asian grocers or, if you are based in the UK, Bold Bean Co Queen Carlin Peas are a great substitute. Freshly grated coconut is traditionally used to make a paste, but I have opted for coconut milk which is more readily available. This curry is often served for breakfast in Kerala alongside string hoppers (also known as *idiyappam*), appam or dosa – but you can enjoy it with chapati or paratha too.

1. Heat the coconut oil in a pan and add the fennel seeds, mustard seeds and fresh curry leaves. Stir for 20 seconds and then add the onion and salt. Cook on a low heat for 4 minutes, then add the grated garlic and ginger and cook for a further 2 minutes.

2. Add the ground spices, followed by the tomatoes. After a minute, add the chickpeas or carlin peas, coconut milk and water. Simmer gently on a low heat for 10 minutes.

3. In a small tempering or frying pan, heat the coconut oil, mustard seeds, curry leaves and dried red chilli. Allow to sizzle for 10 to 15 seconds and then pour the tempering onto the curry and mix well.

4. Taste to check the seasoning and adjust as required. This curry is great alongside the Aloo Dum on page 168 and either Mughal Sheermal (page 238) or Goan Pao (page 140).

Notes: To 'temper' spices means to briefly fry them in hot oil or ghee before pouring them onto the finished dish. Tempering pans are small metal pans, about the size of half a coconut. If you can't find either black chickpeas or carlin peas, tinned or jarred regular yellow chickpeas will work equally well here.

Keralan Beef Fry

Preparation time: 10 minutes
Cooking time: 50 minutes (or 30
minutes in pressure cooker, see notes
on page 9)
Serves 4-6

2 tbsp coconut oil

1 stem of fresh or frozen curry leaves
(about 15 leaves)

2 onions, thinly sliced

3 fresh green chillies, sliced

2 tbsp thinly sliced fresh, frozen or
dehydrated coconut

1 heaped tsp finely grated garlic

1 heaped tsp finely grated fresh ginger

900g beef fillet tail (or similar soft cuts),
cut into 1.5-inch pieces

1 tsp fine salt

1 tsp white vinegar, or coconut vinegar
if you can find it

1 tsp Kashmiri chilli powder

½ tsp ground turmeric

½ tsp freshly ground black pepper

2 tbsp ground coriander

1 tsp garam masala

For the tempering

2 tbsp coconut oil

4 shallots, thinly sliced

1 tbsp thinly sliced coconut

1 stem of fresh curry leaves

½ tsp freshly ground black pepper

This absolute classic known as 'beef roast' or beef *ularthiyathu* is typically made in a pressure cooker, which saves a lot of time. As pressure cookers are not as commonly used in the UK and US, I'm using a stove top method here, which does take longer but tastes equally delicious. The cut of meat that you choose is important and shouldn't be one that requires a long, slow cook as this version is still relatively quick – I suggest using fillet tail. This is a dry dish, so it doesn't have a gravy.

1. In a large casserole pot, bring the coconut oil to a medium heat. Add the curry leaves, onions, fresh green chillies and sliced coconut. Stir for 4 minutes and then add the garlic and ginger. Cook for a further 2 minutes.

2. Now add the beef and salt and allow the beef to lightly brown on all sides over the next 5 minutes. Stir intermittently to help it bronze evenly.

3. Add the vinegar, Kashmiri chilli powder, turmeric, black pepper and ground coriander to the pot, mix well and then pour in enough water to just cover the beef.

4. Bring to the boil and then simmer on a medium heat for the next 30 to 40 minutes, uncovered – do not place a lid on the pan. If the water has not completely evaporated by this time, cook for another 10 minutes.

5. Meanwhile, in a separate small pan or a tempering pan if you have one, heat the coconut oil and then add the shallots, sliced coconut, curry leaves and black pepper. Stir over a medium to high heat until the shallots and coconut are lightly bronzed – this should only take a minute or two.

6. Pour the contents of the pan over the beef and mix well. Taste to check the seasoning and add more salt if required.

7. Finally, fold the garam masala into the beef and serve.

Keralan Garam Masala

Preparation time: 10 minutes
Cooking time: 10-15 minutes
Makes 1 small pot

2 tbsp fennel seeds

2-inch piece of cinnamon or cassia bark

10 green cardamom pods, left whole

½ tsp whole black peppercorns

3 leaves of a star anise

½ mace blade

6 cloves

½ tsp grated nutmeg

Every Indian household has their own treasured family recipe for garam masala. In the north of India, they differ wildly from those in the south when it comes to which spices are included. In Sanskrit, the word garam literally means 'warm or hot' and masala means 'blend of spices'. It is not hot with chilli but instead uses warming spices such as cinnamon, cloves and nutmeg. Garam masala is often used towards the end of cooking so that the flavours and aromas linger longer in the dish. This one is typical in Keralan cuisine.

1. Warm a dry frying pan on a medium heat and add all the ingredients except the grated nutmeg. Move everything around the pan for 1 to 2 minutes to awaken the spices.

2. Transfer the toasted spices to a bowl and leave to cool before grinding them into a fine powder in a spice grinder or with a pestle and mortar.

3. Stir in the grated nutmeg, mix well and then store the masala in a sealed, sterilised jar.

Notes: If you are blending the spices by hand with a pestle and mortar, remove the husks of the cardamom pods, leaving just the seeds, as this will make it easier to blend into a powder.

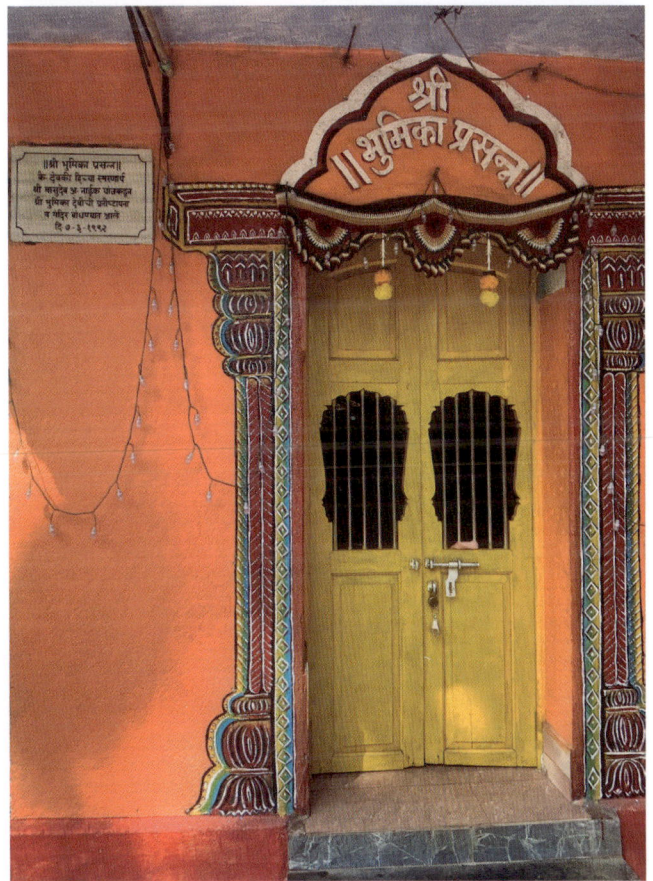

Prawn Fry

Preparation time: 20 minutes
Cooking time: 25 minutes
Serves 4

4 kokum (see notes)

150ml boiling water

2 tbsp coconut oil

5 garlic cloves, roughly chopped

3 shallots, finely chopped

2-inch piece (30g) of fresh ginger, peeled and roughly chopped

1-2 stems of fresh or frozen curry leaves (approx. 15-30 leaves)

1 large or 2 small red onions, finely chopped

1 tsp fine salt

1 tsp ground turmeric

1 tsp Kashmiri chilli powder

2 medium tomatoes, roughly chopped

500g large prawns, deveined and shelled

1 tsp freshly ground black pepper

Back in 2016, I had the pleasure of staying on Philip Kutty's farm in the backwaters of Kerala. The family are Syrian Christians and each day they would prepare delicious home-cooked meals for their guests. In the evening, Aniamma would teach us how to cook the recipes and this dish, known locally as *chemmeen olarthiathu*, is one that we ate during that stay. It's meant to be rather dry, other than the light coating from the tomatoes and spices.

1. Begin by soaking the kokum in the boiling water for 20 minutes. Meanwhile, heat the coconut oil in a wide pan and then add the garlic, shallots, ginger and curry leaves.

2. After a minute, add the onions and salt. Allow everything to soften and lightly bronze over the next 6 to 8 minutes.

3. Stir in the ground turmeric and Kashmiri chilli powder, then add the tomatoes and allow them to soften over the next 3 to 4 minutes.

4. Add the prawns and keep them moving around the pan so they are coated in all the spices and aromatics.

5. After 3 minutes, add the kokum along with the soaking water and continue to cook gently for the next 5 minutes. Finally, add the black pepper and then the prawn fry is ready to serve.

Notes: Kokum is a fruit from the mangosteen family, found in southern states of India. It's similar to tamarind in that it has a sour and fruity flavour. After soaking, it's added to curries, especially fish curries, to introduce sweet and sour notes. Outside of India, they are easily sourced online in dried form.

Whole Fish Pollichathu

Preparation time: 15 minutes
Cooking time: 30 minutes
Serves 4

4 whole small or medium sea bream/
sea bass/pomfret, gutted and cleaned

2 tbsp coconut oil

For the marinade

1 tsp fine salt

1 tsp finely grated fresh ginger

1 tsp finely grated garlic

½ tsp freshly ground black pepper

½ tsp Kashmiri chilli powder

½ tsp ground turmeric

Juice of ½ a lemon

For the masala

2 tbsp coconut oil

1 stem of fresh or frozen curry leaves
(about 15 leaves)

2 green chillies, halved lengthways

5 banana shallots, finely sliced

1 tsp ground coriander

½ tsp ground turmeric

½ tsp Kashmiri chilli powder

½ tsp freshly ground black pepper

½ tsp fine salt

2 tomatoes, roughly chopped

200ml thin coconut milk

To cook and serve

4 large pieces of baking paper or
banana leaf, to wrap the fish

Kitchen string, to tie the parcels

Extra fresh curry leaves

4 tbsp coconut oil

This is a classic Syrian Christian dish, made with pearl spot fish or karameen which are commonly found in the backwaters of Kerala. Pomfret is also often used but in the UK, I like to use sea bass or sea bream. Pollichathu means to fry or grill and there are a few simple steps before you wrap the masala and the fish in baking paper, or a banana leaf if you can find them, to cook it this way – although at home you can oven-bake the fish parcels if you prefer.

1. Begin by carving 3 or 4 slits on each side of the fish.

2. Combine all the marinade ingredients in a bowl and mix well to form a paste.

3. Coat the fish in the marinade, pushing it into the slits to help the flavours permeate.

4. In a non-stick frying pan, heat the coconut oil and add the fish. If you need to do this in more than one batch, add a little more coconut oil to the pan. Fry the fish on both sides for 3 to 4 minutes in total and then remove from the pan.

5. Use the same pan to make the masala. Heat the coconut oil and then add the curry leaves, green chillies and shallots. Keep everything moving around the pan to soften for 4 minutes and then add the ground spices and salt. Mix well and then add the tomatoes. Let them soften to a mush over the next 2 to 3 minutes.

6. Add the coconut milk and simmer until absorbed into the masala. Transfer the contents of the pan to a bowl and set aside.

7. If you are using banana leaf rather than baking paper, remove the spines of the leaf and cut 4 equal pieces big enough to wrap your fish in, then place over a heat source (such as the flame on a gas hob) for a few seconds so it softens and becomes easier to fold.

8. Dollop a spoonful of the masala into the centre of each piece of baking paper or banana leaf and spread it out evenly. Place the fish on top and then top with another dollop of masala. If you have some fresh curry leaves to spare, place a few on top.

9. Fold the baking paper or banana leaf over the fish into a parcel and tie with kitchen string. You can now either fry or bake the fish parcels. To bake, preheat your oven to 190°C/170°C fan/375°F/Gas 5 and place the parcels on a baking tray in the centre for 15 minutes. To fry, heat a little coconut oil in the same non-stick frying pan you used earlier and then place the parcels in the pan (you may need to do this in batches). Cook for 5 minutes on each side, 10 minutes in total. Place a lid on the pan to help steam the fish.

10. Once cooked, place a parcel onto each plate and let the diner open up their individual fish for a delicious treat.

Notes: I like to serve this with steamed basmati rice and Allegra's Kachumber Salad (see page 76). The thin coconut milk I use here is the watery liquid that often separates from the solids in a 400ml tin of coconut milk. If you find that your tin of coconut milk hasn't separated, simply add 200ml of the liquid and save the rest for another recipe.

Chicken Stew

Preparation time: 10 minutes
Cooking time: 40 minutes
Serves 4-6

Known in Kerala as *ishtew* or *ishtoo*, this recipe is similar to a Western stew in temperament but the addition of spices gives it added flair and complexity. The base note is coconut milk, providing a very delicate aroma that will appeal to all. It is a great curry to make if you have vegetables that need using up.

3 tbsp coconut oil

1 stem of fresh or frozen curry leaves (about 15 leaves)

2-inch piece of cinnamon or cassia bark

2 star anise

4 cloves

4 green cardamom pods

2 large onions, finely sliced

1 tsp fine salt

3 garlic cloves, roughly chopped

2-inch piece (30g) of fresh ginger, peeled and finely sliced into batons

1kg skinless chicken thighs and breast, cut into bite-size pieces

500g vegetables, cut into bite-size pieces

2 fresh green chillies, halved lengthways

½ tsp freshly ground black pepper

½ tsp ground turmeric

1 x 400ml tin of coconut milk

200ml water

1 tsp garam masala

1. Begin by heating the coconut oil in a large pan. Add the curry leaves and whole spices, stirring for 30 seconds to infuse the oil with their aromatic flavours.

2. Add the sliced onions and salt to the pan, then allow to lightly bronze over the next 6 minutes.

3. Add the garlic and ginger, cook for another couple of minutes, then add the chicken. Fold it into all the spices and aromatics, then let it start to seal for 3 to 4 minutes before adding the vegetables.

4. Add the fresh chillies, black pepper and ground turmeric, then lower the heat before stirring in the coconut milk and water. Simmer the stew gently for 25 minutes, by which time the chicken will have cooked, and the vegetables nicely softened.

5. Taste to check the seasoning, adding more salt if needed, and then fold in the garam masala. Serve with steamed rice or kallappam (see page 102).

Notes: For the vegetables, I'd recommend choosing a minimum of two from the following: carrot, cauliflower, potato, fine green beans, squash, courgette.

Keralan Ripe Mango Curry

Preparation time: 20 minutes
Cooking time: 15 minutes
Serves 4-6

3 large ripe mangoes (600g after peeling and destoning – see notes)

500ml water

1 tsp fine salt

½ tsp ground turmeric

150ml full-fat Greek yoghurt, stirred to remove lumps

½ tsp fine sugar or jaggery (optional)

For the coconut paste

50g desiccated or freshly grated coconut

1 green chilli, roughly chopped

1 tsp cumin seeds

50ml water

For the tempering

1 tsp coconut oil

1 tsp black or brown mustard seeds

1 stem of fresh or frozen curry leaves (about 15 leaves)

1-2 dried whole red chillies, broken in half

This recipe may initially surprise you, but ripe mango curry with a lightly spiced coconut gravy is a revelation. A favourite among Syrian Christians in Kerala, known locally as *pazha manga* (which means ripe mango), it is simple to prepare and a lovely alternative way to enjoy ripe mangoes. Typically the smaller mangoes found in Kerala would be peeled and used whole (without removing the stones) in this dish, but if you can only find larger ones they can be destoned and chopped into large chunks instead. I am fortunate enough to live near several Asian grocers who stock hundreds of boxes of mangoes when they are in season, though larger supermarkets also stock delicious mangoes which will work well.

1. First, peel your mangoes and either leave them whole if small or cut into chunks and remove the stones if large. Place into a pan and cover with the water. Add the salt and turmeric, then simmer gently for 10 minutes. The mango should hold its shape and not become mushy so make sure it doesn't overcook.

2. Meanwhile, place all the ingredients for the coconut paste into a wet grinder and blitz until smooth. Add a little more water if required to form a paste.

3. After the mango has simmered for 10 minutes, lower the heat and stir in the smooth Greek yoghurt. Make sure the pan stays on a low heat as otherwise the yoghurt will split.

4. Add the coconut paste to the pan and stir it into the mango and yoghurt mixture.

5. Heat the coconut oil in the smallest pan you own, or a tempering pan if you have one. When hot, add the mustard seeds, curry leaves and dried red chilli. Move around the pan in the oil for 10 seconds – they will begin to splutter so be careful – and then pour the tempering over the curry and gently fold in.

6. Taste the curry to check the seasoning, adding the sugar or jaggery and more salt if required. When you are happy with the flavours, serve with steamed basmati rice.

Notes: Badami or Kesar mangoes work well in this dish, though the larger standard variety you find at regular supermarkets is fine, peeled and cut into large chunks with the stones removed. If you have smaller mangoes, simply peel them and keep them whole without removing the stones, using one small mango per person.

Duck Roast

Preparation time: 10 minutes
Cooking time: 50 minutes – 1 hour 10 minutes, depending on method
Serves 6

3 tbsp coconut oil

15 thin slices of fresh or dried coconut, cut into 1-inch pieces

50g fresh ginger, peeled and cut into thin batons

10 garlic cloves, roughly chopped

10 shallots, sliced

2 medium red onions, sliced

1 tsp fine salt

2 stems of fresh or frozen curry leaves (about 15 leaves each)

2 medium tomatoes, roughly chopped

2 heaped tsp freshly ground black pepper

2 tsp ground coriander

1 tsp ground turmeric

1 tsp ground fennel

½ tsp Kashmiri chilli powder

1.8kg duck legs, skin on and bone in (6-8 legs)

3 fresh green chillies, slit lengthways

1 tsp garam masala

300ml water

This much-loved Syrian Christian dish is known as *tharavu* roast and is much loved in the state of Kerala. It's often prepared on special occasions such as Christmas, Easter and at weddings. If you have a pressure cooker, I really urge you to use it here as it not only speeds up the cooking time but also makes the meat so tender and leaves it falling off the bone.

1. Heat the coconut oil in a casserole pot or pressure cooker and when hot, add the coconut slices. Move them around for 3 to 4 minutes until lightly bronzed.

2. Add the ginger, garlic and shallots to the pot and stir for 2 minutes before adding the red onions, salt and 1 stem of curry leaves.

3. Allow the onions to bronze over the next 8 to 10 minutes, stirring intermittently to avoid anything catching on the bottom. If it does start to stick, add a splash of water.

4. Now add the tomatoes and allow to soften for a couple of minutes. Stir in the black pepper, coriander, turmeric, fennel and Kashmiri chilli powder, then add the duck legs. Give everything a good stir to coat the duck in all the spices and aromatics.

5. After 5 minutes, add the fresh green chillies, garam masala and water. If you are going to pressure cook the duck, close the lid and cook for 25 minutes on a high heat. If you are using a regular casserole dish, cover with the lid and cook over a medium heat for 45 to 50 minutes, stirring intermittently.

6. After this time, check that the duck meat is lovely and soft. If it isn't, continue to cook for another 10 to 15 minutes on a low heat. If the dish is looking very dry at this stage, add a splash more water to help the meat soften. Taste to check the seasoning and add more salt if required.

7. Finally, add the remaining curry leaves and stir into the dish just before serving it with steamed basmati rice and Allegra's Kachumber Salad (see page 76).

Kallappam – Rice Pancakes

Preparation time: 5 hours to overnight
Cooking time: 20 minutes
Makes 15

For the kurukku (paste)
50g rice flour
300ml water

For the batter
250g rice flour
60g shredded fresh or desiccated coconut, or coconut milk
1 tsp easy bake/instant yeast
2 round shallots, peeled
2 garlic cloves, peeled
2 tbsp caster sugar
1 tsp cumin seeds
1 tsp salt
200ml water
1 tsp coconut oil per pancake

These tasty pancakes are traditionally made with soaked rice that is then ground into a batter. For speed, and to encourage you to have a go at making them, I have opted for rice flour. In South India, the sap from coconut palms – called *kallu* – is used for the fermentation but as it's not easy to source here, I've substituted it with yeast. While these pancakes are typically eaten for breakfast, I like them for lunch or supper alongside Aloo Dum (page 168), Chicken Curry Himalayan Style (page 154) or Keralan Beef Fry (page 88).

1. Begin by making a thick paste, known as kurukku. Place the rice flour in a medium pan and add the water. Use a spatula to mix them together over a medium heat until a thick paste forms. This will take around 5 minutes. Turn off the heat and set aside.

2. In a blender, blitz the rice flour, coconut or coconut milk and yeast to a thick paste. Now add the kurukku paste along with the shallots, garlic cloves, sugar, cumin seeds and salt. Add the water and blitz to form a smooth batter.

3. If you live in a cooler climate, heat your oven for a couple of minutes and then turn it off completely but leave the light on. This will create a warm place for the batter to ferment. Pour the batter into a large bowl, cover and place in the oven for 5 hours or overnight. If you live in a warmer climate, simply leave the bowl on the side uncovered.

4. Once fermented, the batter should be frothy. Give it a good stir and heat a frying pan, tawa or flat griddle pan once you are ready to cook the pancakes.

5. Add a teaspoon of coconut oil to the pan or tawa and then use a ladle to pour a little of the batter into the pan to create a pancake roughly the size of a saucer.

6. When you see small holes begin to form on the surface of the pancake, use a spatula to carefully turn it over. Let it bronze lightly on both sides, then transfer to a warm plate and repeat with more coconut oil and the rest of the batter.

7. You can use the batter over a few days, so make as many pancakes as you need and leave the remaining batter in the fridge, covered, until you are ready to make more.

Notes: If you prefer to use active dry yeast, you need to activate it before use with a teaspoon of sugar and a little warm (not hot!) water. Combine in a small bowl and leave for 10 minutes.

Prawn Peera

Preparation time: 10 minutes
Cooking time: 10 minutes
Serves 4

100g freshly grated coconut or desiccated coconut

8 round shallots, 4 finely sliced and 4 roughly chopped

1-inch piece (15g) of fresh ginger, peeled and roughly chopped

4 garlic cloves, roughly chopped

1 fresh green chilli, roughly chopped

½ - 1 tsp Kashmiri chilli powder, to taste

½ tsp ground turmeric

600g large prawns, peeled, cleaned and deveined

3 tbsp coconut oil

1 stem of fresh or frozen curry leaves (about 15 leaves), plus extra to serve

3 kudampuli, soaked in a little warm water for 10 minutes (or tamarind pulp – see notes)

3 dried whole red chillies

Fine salt, to taste

50ml water

A very quick and simple dry dish made with prawns and coconut. The actual cooking time is under 15 minutes, which makes it a great option for a midweek meal. While you can do all the chopping and slicing by hand, if you have a wet grinder, I encourage you to use that to prepare the coconut mix. Earthenware pots over a cooking fire are traditionally used to make this dish, but a pan on a modern stove will work equally well.

1. Place the coconut in a wet grinder along with the 4 chopped shallots, ginger, garlic, fresh chilli, Kashmiri chilli powder and ground turmeric. Add a splash of water and blitz briefly a couple of times so that it all comes together. A roughly blended mixture rather than a smooth paste is what you're looking for here.

2. Without turning on the heat, add the blitzed ingredients to a pan along with the prawns, 2 tablespoons of the coconut oil, the curry leaves, kudampuli along with their soaking water, dried chillies and salt. Use your hands to completely combine the ingredients.

3. Turn on the heat, add the water to the pan and cover for 5 minutes. After this time, give the mixture a good stir and then cover with the lid again to cook for a further 5 minutes.

4. Add a few extra fresh curry leaves and drizzle the remaining coconut oil over the prawn peera to serve. Enjoy with some freshly steamed rice.

Notes: Kudampuli – also known as Malabar tamarind – is similar to but not the same as kokum. Both have a tart flavour but kudampuli is sourer. They are from the same family but the kudampuli has more grooves in its skin and is commonly used in South Indian cuisine while kokum is used slightly further north in Goan cuisine. Both can be found online in the UK. You can replace the kudampuli here with 30g of soaked and strained tamarind pulp, 2 teaspoons of tamarind paste or 1 teaspoon of tamarind concentrate if needed.

Spiced Cassava

Preparation time: 15 minutes
Cooking time: 25-30 minutes
Serves 4-6

1kg cassava

1½ tsp fine salt

2 tbsp coconut oil

1 tsp black or brown mustard seeds

1 tsp cumin seeds

2 dried whole red chillies, broken in
half, or ½ tsp dried chilli flakes

1 stem of fresh or frozen curry leaves
(about 15 leaves)

1 small red onion or 4 shallots, finely
sliced

3 garlic cloves, finely chopped

60g fresh coconut, coarsely blended
(or desiccated coconut if you cannot
find fresh)

1 fresh green chilli, finely chopped
(optional)

1 tsp ground turmeric

400ml water

You may have these seen large, dark brown, root-like vegetables at larger supermarkets in the UK and wondered what they were or what to do with them. You may be more familiar with the starch extracted from them which is called tapioca. However, cassava is a major food crop in Africa and South America and also eaten in India, especially in the south. In Kerala, they are known as *kappa* and this local recipe is called *kappa puzhukku*. Cassava were thought of as poor man's food but over the years they have become popular across the social divides and have now made it onto the menus of restaurants and hotels. If you can't find them anywhere, white potatoes can be used instead.

1. Begin by peeling the cassava, removing the brown outer skin and the pinkish skin underneath so you are left with the white centre part. Roughly chop this into 1-inch cubes. Wash well, then cover with fresh water in a pan, add half a teaspoon of the salt and boil for 10 to 15 minutes until soft. Drain the cooked cassava and set aside.

2. Heat the coconut oil in a large, wide pan on a medium to low heat. When hot, add the mustard seeds and cumin seeds – be careful as they can splutter in the oil.

3. Next add the dried red chillies and curry leaves followed by the red onion or shallot, garlic and remaining salt. Allow everything to lightly bronze over the next 4 minutes or so.

4. Add the coconut, fresh green chilli if using and ground turmeric to the pan. Mix well and after a couple of minutes, add the prepared cassava and 400ml of water. Simmer for a further 5 minutes, then mash some of the cassava into the liquid to give it a thicker consistency.

5. Taste to check the salt levels and when you are happy with the flavour, it's ready to serve alongside meat or fish curries.

Sweetly Spiced Rice Flakes

Preparation time: 5 minutes
Cooking time: 15 minutes
Makes a large batch that keeps for a month in a sealed container

1 tbsp ghee or coconut oil

40g unsalted cashew nuts

60g sultanas or roughly chopped dates

2 tbsp raw chana dal/Bengal gram

1 tbsp black sesame seeds

1 tbsp coconut oil

80g finely grated fresh or frozen coconut, or desiccated coconut

200ml water

120g jaggery or muscovado sugar

1 tsp ground cardamom

1 tsp ground ginger

250g white or brown rice flakes (also known as *poha* or *powa*)

Known as *aval vilayichathu*, this Keralan teatime snack is often eaten alongside banana. While not exclusively eaten by the Syrian Christians, it is much loved by this community. The recipe is easy to prepare and delicious alongside a mug of hot chai. Rice flakes, which are white or brown and similar to but softer than cornflakes, are found in Asian grocers, as is jaggery, an unrefined cane sugar, although it can be substituted with muscovado sugar.

1. In a large, wide pan or wok, heat the ghee or oil and then add the unsalted cashew nuts. Stir for a minute before adding the sultanas or dates and chana dal.

2. Keep everything moving around in the pan for 1 to 2 minutes and then add the black sesame seeds. After 10 seconds, use a spatula to transfer all the ingredients to a bowl and set aside.

3. Using the same pan, heat the coconut oil and then add the coconut and let it lightly bronze for a minute. Remove and place in a separate bowl.

4. Again in the same pan, combine the water and jaggery or muscovado sugar. Bring to a simmer and allow the jaggery or sugar to completely dissolve before adding the coconut. Stir for 30 seconds and then add the cashew nut mixture.

5. Next, add the ground cardamom and ginger. Stir well and then gradually add the rice flakes, coating them in all the spiced sugary goodness. Keep moving this mixture around the pan for a minute until browned, then remove from the heat.

6. Once cooled, store the rice flakes in a sealed container for up to a month.

Notes: Traditionally, these spiced rice flakes are served as an afternoon snack along with some masala chai. I prefer to make them into a delicately sweet, chewy, crunchy and light dessert to serve at the end of a meal – simply layer a dollop of Greek yoghurt, a few tablespoons of the spiced flakes and some slices of fresh banana in a bowl.

I like to use the small nuggets of jaggery you can buy from Asian grocers for this recipe. Do adjust the quantity of jaggery or sugar to suit your own sweet tooth.

Coconut Pancakes

Preparation time: 10 minutes
Cooking time: 10-15 minutes
Makes 5 large or 10 small pancakes

Coconut or neutral oil

For the filling

50g freshly grated coconut, or desiccated coconut

3 tbsp condensed milk

1 tbsp dark muscovado sugar or jaggery

¼ tsp ground green cardamom

For the batter

1 x 400ml tin of coconut milk

200g plain white flour, sifted

¼ tsp ground turmeric

¼ tsp fine salt

2 eggs, whisked

80-100ml water

For the sauce

3 tbsp condensed milk

1 tbsp coconut cream

¼ tsp ground cinnamon

There is a wonderful book by Lathika George called *The Kerala Kitchen* which focuses on recipes and recollections from the Syrian Christians in South India. One recipe that caught my eye was *madakappams*, or coconut pancakes. They are not just a Syrian Christian sweet treat, however. According to my mother-in-law, who is a Bengali Hindu from Kolkata, they are eaten in Bangladesh and West Bengal too, known there as *pati shapta*. Apparently, they are devoured particularly at the end of the winter, in late January. My recipe is a fusion of Lathika's version and the one you find in Bengal – I'm sure you will enjoy this delicate sweet treat.

1. Mix the ingredients for the filling together in a bowl and set aside.

2. In a large bowl, combine the ingredients for the batter, adjusting the quantity of water as needed to create a consistency that's neither too thick nor too thin.

3. Heat a non-stick frying pan and use kitchen paper to wipe a little coconut oil or neutral oil around the bottom of the pan. Keep the heat low.

4. Use a jug or ladle to pour a little of the pancake batter into the pan and tilt the pan to spread it out evenly, in the same way you would with a traditional flat English pancake.

5. Cover the pan with a lid and leave for a minute. It is not necessary to flip these pancakes.

6. Check that the top of the pancake has firmed up and then gently slide it out the pan and onto a warm plate.

7. Place a couple of teaspoons of the filling along one edge of the pancake and then gently roll up so that it looks like a cigar. Repeat Steps 4 to 6 until all the batter and filling have been used up.

8. To make the sauce, simply combine all the ingredients in a small pan, heat for no more than a minute or two, then drizzle over the pancakes to serve.

Goan Portuguese

The Portuguese invaded Goa under the leadership of Afonso de Albuquerque in 1510, fighting the ruling Sultanate of Bijapur. Portugal continued to rule over the smallest Indian state on the west coast for just over 450 years; while India gained its independence from Britain in 1947, Goa remained under Portuguese control until 1961.

The Portuguese brought many influences to the region that changed Goan food, culture, architecture and religion and much of that influence is still evident today. Before the Portuguese arrived in India, chillies, potatoes, tomatoes, pomegranates, papayas, custard apples, corn, pineapples, pumpkins, squash and cashew nuts were not known to the local population. Having already made inroads into South America, particularly Brazil, the Portuguese were able to bring their culinary discoveries to India. Being based in Goa gave the Portuguese a strategic vantage point along the coast of the Arabian Sea to oversee the lucrative Eastern spice trade, which had previously been dominated by Arab and Venetian merchants. Goan rule also allowed the Portuguese to spread Catholicism among the local population, who were largely Hindu at the time and subsequently forced to convert, flee the state or face execution. The impact of this can still be felt throughout Goa, where the majority of inhabitants are practising Catholics at the numerous churches and chapels across the state, embedding Portuguese influence in its social fabric.

The flavours of Goan food are very distinct from any other state in India. The new ingredients and styles of cooking introduced by the Portuguese merged with the local cuisine to create a unique blend that is still very popular to this day. Prior to the Portuguese arriving in Goa, the native population ate mostly vegetable and fish dishes, the latter owing to their coastal location and the many tributaries meandering through the state. Chicken and goat were eaten, but pork and beef were off the menu until new food habits began to take hold during the widespread conversion from Hinduism to Catholicism. Today the Goan diet is meat-heavy, with pork the most commonly consumed, and the Portuguese addition of vinegar to many curries gives them a signature sour note. Vindaloo is perhaps one of the best known Goan exports, though its spice level would vary hugely depending on the cook. An authentic vindaloo consisted of little more than meat, wine and garlic — but the Indian take on this dish added plenty of heat to create the spicy curry we are much more familiar with in the UK. I've included a Goan Portuguese version in the recipes that follow alongside other delicious dishes from this unique coastal state.

Arroz Pulao

Preparation time: 10 minutes
Cooking time: 20 minutes
Serves 4

200g basmati rice

3 tbsp vegetable, sunflower or rapeseed oil

8 black peppercorns

5 cloves

1 Indian bay leaf

2-inch piece of cinnamon or cassia bark

1 medium white onion, finely chopped

2 medium tomatoes, finely chopped

1 chicken or vegetable bouillon or stock cube

½ tsp ground turmeric

400ml warm water

70g frozen peas

Salt, to taste

Arroz means rice in Portuguese and this arroz pulao is much loved and served all over the state of Goa. With the arrival of the Portuguese, tomatoes were introduced into India and began to be used in local dishes. This pulao can accompany many of the dishes in this book, not only those in this chapter.

1. Place the rice in a bowl and cover with cold water. Gently wash and drain the rice, then repeat a couple of times. Cover with fresh water and set aside while you continue with the next steps.

2. Heat the oil in a pan on a medium heat and when hot, add all the whole spices – the black peppercorns, cloves, Indian bay leaf and cinnamon or cassia bark. Move them around the pan for a minute before adding the onion.

3. Allow the onion to soften over the next 3 minutes before adding the tomatoes. Allow them to soften and break down with the onion for a further 2 minutes.

4. Crumble in the bouillon or stock cube and mix well with the ingredients in the pan, then stir in the ground turmeric.

5. Drain the rice, then add it to the pan and gently fold in, being careful not to break the grains. Cover with the warm water and then add the frozen peas. Gradually bring to the boil and taste the liquid at this stage to check the salt levels, adding salt if required. I often find store-bought stock cubes salty enough but if you are adding fresh stock, you may need to add a little salt to taste. Stir and then cover with a lid for 10 to 12 minutes.

6. Remove the lid and use a fork to gently bring the rice away from the sides of the pan. If you notice a little liquid remaining at the bottom of the pan, cook for another minute or two on a low heat with the lid on.

7. Once all the liquid has been absorbed, turn off the heat and let the rice steam for a few minutes with the lid on. To serve, gently fluff the rice with a fork and remove the whole spices (or as many as you can find).

Fish Curry

Preparation time: 20 minutes
Cooking time: 20 minutes
Serves 4-6

½ tsp fine salt

700g salmon, cod, tuna or another firm fish, cut into 2-2.5-inch pieces

30g tamarind pulp or 2 tsp tamarind paste or 1 tsp tamarind concentrate

2 tbsp coconut oil

1 tsp black mustard seeds

2 fresh green chillies, slit lengthways on the diagonal

15 fresh or frozen curry leaves

1 onion, thinly sliced

1 tsp salt, or to taste

2 medium tomatoes, roughly chopped

1 tbsp tomato paste

200ml water

1-2 tsp brown or caster sugar

For the wet masala

80g grated fresh or desiccated coconut

3-4 dried Kashmiri chillies, or 1-2 tsp red chilli flakes

5 garlic cloves, kept whole

1 tbsp coriander seeds

1 tbsp cumin seeds

1 tsp ground turmeric

150ml cold water

Being a coastal state, fish has always been central to the cuisine of Goa. Kingfish, pomfret, shark, tuna, sardines and mackerel are most commonly eaten. Chillies and tomatoes were introduced to India with the arrival of Vasco da Gama and the Portuguese in the sixteenth century and keenly adopted into the local cuisine. This curry offers sour notes from the addition of tamarind, balanced with tomatoes and chillies that add sweetness and heat.

1. Begin by sprinkling the salt over the fish in a bowl, then setting aside.

2. If using tamarind pulp, place in a small bowl and cover with warm water. Leave it to soak for 10 minutes, then use your whole hand to break it up completely. Strain through a sieve into a bowl and use the back of a spoon to push through all the pulp. Discard the fibrous parts and seeds.

3. Place all the wet masala ingredients into a fine blender or wet grinder and whizz to form a loose paste. It won't be completely smooth, but the coriander and cumin seeds should have broken down and blended well with the rest of the ingredients.

4. Heat the coconut oil in a large pan and add the black mustard seeds, fresh chillies, curry leaves, onion and salt. Allow the onion to soften and very lightly bronze over the next 5 minutes.

5. Add the tomatoes and move everything around the pan for a couple of minutes before adding the wet masala. Keep the heat low, stirring to avoid it catching on the bottom.

6. Add the tamarind pulp, paste or concentrate along with the tomato paste and stir well before adding the water.

7. Add a little sugar and taste to check if the flavours are to your liking. Add a little more sugar or salt to suit your preferences.

8. Gently bring the sauce to the boil, then add the fish and lower the heat slightly. Simmer for 5 to 7 minutes. Top up with a little more water if you wish, depending on how loose you would like the consistency of the curry to be.

9. Serve alongside steamed basmati rice.

Notes: It is important to use a fine blender, wet grinder or Nutribullet in Step 3 so that the coriander and cumin seeds break down. A food processor will not blend the masala sufficiently. If you want to make this curry for just 4 people, I'd recommend reducing the quantity of fish to 500g but keeping all the other ingredient quantities the same.

Tamarind pulp, as opposed to paste or concentrate, is available at Asian grocery stores and some large supermarkets, usually found in block form wrapped in cellophane. It stores in the fridge for months. I tend to buy it in this form but tamarind paste is equally good. If you buy tamarind concentrate, use with caution as it's much stronger in flavour.

Goan Frijoada

Preparation time: 10 minutes
Cooking time: 40 minutes
Serves 4

2 tbsp vegetable, sunflower or rapeseed oil

4 cloves

2-inch piece of cinnamon or cassia bark

2 green cardamom pods, opened

1 large onion, finely diced

2 fresh green chillies, halved lengthways

1 heaped tsp finely grated garlic

1 heaped tsp finely grated fresh ginger

1 large tomato, diced

1 tsp smoked paprika

½ tsp chilli powder

½ tsp ground turmeric

½ tsp freshly ground black pepper

1 tsp tomato paste

200g chorizo, sausages or Goan sausage, diced into ½ inch cubes

300g boneless pork shoulder or belly, diced into ½ inch cubes (optional)

400g jar or tin of red kidney beans, drained

1 tsp salt, or to taste

200ml water

Wherever the Portuguese had their territories, the cross pollination of textures and flavours followed. Frijoada is considered a national dish of Brazil – a hearty, warming stew that was introduced to Goa by the Portuguese. Goan residents then put their own spin on the dish using local spices. Both pork and beef are traditionally used, but in Goa it is largely pork that is found in the dish. Goans use a specific spiced sausage, which is bright red, sold in bead-like strings and deliciously spiced (not dissimilar to chorizo). Traditionally, other parts of the pig are also added – feet, ear, trotter or heart – but pork belly or shoulder are good substitutes, or you can choose to leave them out entirely. The dish also includes red kidney beans, cow peas or black beans. I opt for jarred or tinned red kidney beans, which work really well.

1. Heat the oil in a pan and then add the cloves, cinnamon or cassia bark and green cardamom pods. Move them around the pan for 30 seconds before adding the onion and fresh green chillies.

2. Keep the pan on a low heat and allow the onion to soften and lightly bronze over the next 5 minutes before adding the garlic and ginger. Stir for a minute before adding the tomato.

3. Next add the ground spices: smoked paprika, chilli powder, turmeric and black pepper. Stir in the tomato paste, then add the chorizo or sausage and diced pork, if using. Give everything a good stir so the spices coat the meat.

4. Simmer for 5 minutes and then add the red kidney beans, salt and water. Stir well, then place a lid on the pan and simmer gently for 20 minutes. Add a little more water if required.

5. Taste to check the salt levels and heat, adjusting according to your preferences. Serve the frijoada with steamed basmati rice or the Goan bread known as pao (see page 140)

Notes: If you are based in the UK, Bold Bean Co Queen Red Beans work really well here. You can also use black beans in this dish for variety.

Chana Ros

Preparation time: 15-20 minutes
Cooking time: 25-30 minutes
Serves 4

For the paste

2 tbsp coconut oil

1 medium onion, sliced

1 fresh or frozen green chilli, or 1 dried whole red chilli (optional)

3 garlic cloves, roughly chopped

1 medium tomato, roughly chopped

40g grated fresh or frozen coconut, or desiccated coconut

4 cloves

5 black peppercorns

1-inch piece of cinnamon or cassia bark

2 tsp coriander seeds

1 tsp fennel seeds

1 tsp ground turmeric

30g tamarind pulp or 2 tsp tamarind paste or 1 tsp tamarind concentrate

300ml water

For the dal

2 tbsp coconut oil

1 tsp black or brown mustard seeds

10 fresh or frozen curry leaves

2 x 400g jars or tins of chickpeas, drained and rinsed

1 large potato, peeled and diced into 1-inch cubes (optional)

400ml water

1 tsp salt, or to taste

½ tsp sugar

½ tsp garam masala

Small handful of coriander leaves, to serve

I ate this comforting and filling chickpea dal in Goa for breakfast on many occasions. It was hearty, delicately spiced and the perfect way to wake up the taste buds. It is worth investing in a wet grinder that makes the paste smooth; for me this is a kitchen essential. In Goa, chana ros is typically eaten alongside a local bread known as *pao* or *poori*, but a bowl of this on its own for breakfast or lunch is more than satisfying.

1. If using tamarind pulp, place in a small bowl and cover with warm water. Leave it to soak for 10 minutes, then use your whole hand to break it up completely. Strain through a sieve into a bowl and use the back of a spoon to push through all the pulp. Discard the fibrous parts and seeds.

2. First, make the paste. In a frying pan, heat the coconut oil and then add the onion and chilli, if using. After 3 minutes, add the garlic.

3. Next, add the tomato and coconut. Move everything around the pan for a couple of minutes to lightly bronze the coconut.

4. Move the ingredients to one side of the pan, add a little more oil and then add all the spices. Toast them for a minute and then mix with the contents of the pan.

5. Turn off the heat and allow to cool slightly before placing the contents of the pan into a wet grinder, adding the tamarind pulp, paste or concentrate and the water. Blitz until you have a smooth paste.

6. Using a wide pan of medium depth, heat the coconut oil for the dal and then add the mustard seeds and curry leaves. They will immediately begin to splutter so keep the heat low.

7. Add the chickpeas, cubed potato (if using) and the blitzed paste along with the water. Simmer gently for 10 minutes, topping up with more water if required to help soften the potato.

8. Add the salt and sugar to balance the flavours. Sprinkle the garam masala on top and stir into the dal. Simmer a little longer until you have a thick gravy.

9. To serve, scatter the chana ros with some fresh coriander leaves.

Notes: Tamarind pulp, as opposed to paste or concentrate, is available at Asian grocery stores and some large supermarkets, usually found in block form wrapped in cellophane. It stores in the fridge for months. I tend to buy it in this form but tamarind paste is equally good. If you buy tamarind concentrate, use with caution as it's much stronger in flavour.

Chicken Cafreal

Preparation time: 15 minutes, plus at least 2 hours marinating
Cooking time: 40 minutes
Serves 4-6

1kg chicken thighs and legs on the bone, or boneless and skinless

1 tsp salt

½ tsp ground turmeric

1 tsp white or cider vinegar

2 tbsp olive oil

For the cafreal masala paste

2 handfuls of fresh coriander, stalks and leaves

1 small handful of fresh mint, stalks removed

2-3 fresh green chillies

8 garlic cloves, peeled

2-inch (30g) piece of fresh ginger

2-inch piece of cinnamon or cassia bark

4 green cardamom pods

6 cloves

1 tsp cumin seeds

1 tsp black peppercorns

1 tsp caster or soft brown sugar

1 tsp white or cider vinegar or lime juice

A much-loved Goan dish that was introduced by the Portuguese via Africa. Caffraria was the name given to the territories along the southeast coast of Africa, colonised by the Portuguese and the British. The Portuguese ruled over Mozambique, and it is likely that the dish migrated to Goa from this region. It is a semi-dry recipe that would work as well on the barbecue as it does in the pan. Traditionally, this recipe would include a splash of local toddy vinegar, but you can replace this with white or cider vinegar or lime juice.

1. First, make some incisions into the chicken pieces to help the full flavours of the marinade seep into the meat. Sprinkle with the salt, ground turmeric and vinegar.

2. Place all the ingredients for the cafreal masala paste in a wet grinder and blitz until smooth. Add a splash of water if required to loosen.

3. Rub the masala paste over the prepared chicken, then cover and leave to marinate for at least 2 hours. If you want to cook it on a barbecue, prepare that in the meantime.

4. Heat the olive oil in a pan and when hot, add the chicken in batches. Do not overcrowd the pan. Leave to bronze for 5 to 7 minutes before turning over and bronzing on the other side. Remove from the pan and repeat with the remaining pieces of chicken.

5. Return all the meat to the pan and add any remaining paste from the tray the chicken was marinating in. Add a splash of water to prevent burning on the bottom of the pan, then cover with a lid and leave to cook for a further 10 minutes.

6. Traditionally, cafreal is eaten with potato wedges or fries and salad. However, it works equally well with Arroz Pulao (see page 114) and Allegra's Kachumber Salad on page 76.

Pork or Pumpkin Vindaloo

Preparation time: 15 minutes
Cooking time: 1 hour 10 minutes for
pork, 40 minutes for pumpkin/squash
Serves 4-6

1 tsp salt

1kg lean pork or pumpkin/squash,
diced into 1-2-inch cubes

2-inch piece of cinnamon or cassia bark

8 dried Kashmiri chillies

9 black peppercorns

8 cloves

10 garlic cloves, peeled

2-inch piece (30g) of fresh ginger

1 tsp cumin seeds

½ tsp black mustard seeds

½ tsp brown sugar

120ml white wine vinegar

2 tbsp vegetable, sunflower or
rapeseed oil

2 medium onions, finely chopped

250ml water

100ml coconut milk (optional)

Vindaloo is probably one of the most well-known curries in the world and one of the most loved across the UK. Traditionally it is cooked with pork, and indeed a pork vindaloo found its way into my first cookbook, which is very different from this recipe. Though it's now renowned for being especially hot, the name comes from the Portuguese *vinha d'alhos* which translates as 'wine and garlic' – these key ingredients were applied to meat along with very few spices, if any. It was the Goans who added their own spicy take on this Portuguese dish and over time it morphed into the decidedly hot curry we know today. On a recent trip to Goa I stayed at the beautiful Figueiredo House, built in 1590 by the Figureirdo family who still reside in the property, and their version of vindaloo was much less spicy but equally moreish. This version also works really well as a vegetarian dish, with pumpkin or butternut squash replacing the pork.

1. If you are using pork, begin by salting it in a large bowl. Place all the whole spices, garlic, ginger, cumin and mustard seeds, sugar and vinegar into a wet grinder and blitz until you have a smooth paste.

2. Pour the paste over the pork and massage in, then cover the bowl and leave to rest in the fridge for a few hours or overnight. If you're short of time, you can skip this step and just add the paste and pork to the pan in Step 3. If you're using pumpkin or squash, there's no need to marinate it so you can also skip this step.

3. Heat the oil in the pan, add the onions and lightly bronze over the next 6 to 8 minutes. If you're using pumpkin or squash, add the paste and stir for a few minutes before adding the cubed veg. If you are cooking with marinated pork, add it to the onions and mix well, then stir fry for 10 minutes before adding the water. For pumpkin or squash, add the water after just a few minutes.

4. At this stage you can either continue to cook on the hob or place the pan in a preheated oven at 200°C/180°C fan/400°F/Gas 6. With either method, it will need 25 to 30 minutes if cooking with veg and 40 minutes if cooking with pork.

5. Although it's not traditional, I often stir in 100ml of coconut milk at the end of the cooking time on a low heat to help balance the spice. I find it creates a lovely balance of salty, sour and sweet flavours but whether to add this or not is totally up to you.

6. Taste the dish to check the salt levels and season as required. If the dish looks too dry, add a splash more water to loosen the sauce.

7. I like to serve this with the Parsi 'Brown' Rice on page 186 and Allegra's Kachumber Salad (see page 76) on the side.

Chicken Xacuti

Preparation time: 15 minutes, plus 1 hour marinating
Cooking time: 40 minutes
Serves 4-6

1kg chicken thighs, cut into bite-size pieces or 1 whole chicken, skinned and cut into 10-12 pieces
1 tsp ground turmeric
1 tsp salt
30g tamarind pulp or 2 tsp tamarind paste or 1 tsp tamarind concentrate
3 tbsp coconut or vegetable oil
1 red onion, finely chopped
3 medium tomatoes, finely diced
250ml water
Fresh coriander, to serve

For the green masala
2-inch piece (30g) of fresh ginger, peeled and roughly chopped
30g fresh coriander, including stalks
2 fresh green chillies, deseeded
10 garlic cloves, peeled
3-4 tbsp cold water

For the xacuti masala
6 dried whole red chillies (use Kashmiri chillies for a milder heat)
2-inch piece of cinnamon or cassia bark
2 green cardamom pods
10 black peppercorns
10 cloves
½ each of star anise and mace blade
1 tbsp white poppy seeds
1 tbsp coriander seeds
½ tsp fenugreek seeds
½ tsp cumin seeds
½ tsp fennel seeds
¼ tsp grated nutmeg

For the coconut masala
1-2 tbsp coconut or vegetable oil
½ onion, roughly chopped
80g fresh or desiccated coconut, finely grated
75ml water

Pronounced 'sha-koo-tee', this Goan speciality is well loved throughout the state of Goa and eaten by the Catholic, Hindu and Muslim communities. In Portugal, the dish is known as *chacuti*. While its origin is more likely to have been Konkan – the coastal region of Maharashtra, Goa and Karnataka – the addition of meat would have been the influence of the Portuguese. I've used chicken but it also works well with a medley of vegetables, such as cauliflower florets, carrots, tomatoes, aubergines and green beans. It may look a chore to make as there are three masalas, but it really is very straightforward and always a crowd pleaser.

1. First, prepare the green masala by blitzing all the ingredients to a smooth paste in a small blender.
2. Place the chicken in a bowl and cover with the green masala, ground turmeric and salt. Cover and chill in the fridge for an hour. Bring back to room temperature before cooking.
3. Next, prepare the xacuti masala. In a dry frying pan, toast all the ingredients except the nutmeg for 1 minute, moving them around to avoid burning. Set aside to cool, then blitz in a spice grinder to form a smooth powder and stir in the nutmeg.
4. Using the same pan, heat the oil for the coconut masala and then add the onion. Allow it to soften before adding the grated coconut. Stir for 3 to 4 minutes until lightly bronzed, then transfer to a blender, add the water and blitz to form a smooth paste.
5. Now that you have prepared all three masalas, you are ready to make the curry. If using tamarind pulp, place in a small bowl and cover with warm water. Leave it to soak for 10 minutes, then use your whole hand to break it up completely. Strain through a sieve into a bowl and use the back of a spoon to push through all the pulp. Discard the fibrous parts and seeds.
6. Heat the oil in a deep, wide saucepan and when hot, add the red onion. Allow it to soften and begin to bronze for around 6 to 8 minutes, then add the tomato and simmer for 2 minutes.
7. Add the marinated chicken, folding it into the onion and tomatoes, then pour in the other two masalas, followed by the tamarind pulp, paste or concentrate. Stir in the 250ml of water, then place a lid on the pan and simmer gently for 30 minutes. At this stage you can continue cooking on the hob or transfer to a preheated oven at 200°C/180°C fan/400°F/Gas 6.
8. Stir intermittently and add more water if it begins to look too dry. Once simmered, check the gravy for seasoning and add a little more salt if required.
9. Cook for a further 10 minutes, by which time some oil will have formed on the top, then serve the xacuti scattered with fresh coriander.

Notes: Tamarind pulp, as opposed to paste or concentrate, is available at Asian grocery stores and some large supermarkets, usually found in block form wrapped in cellophane. It stores in the fridge for months. I tend to buy it in this form but tamarind paste is equally good. If you buy tamarind concentrate, use with caution as it's much stronger in flavour.

Goan Pork Sorpotel

Preparation time: 20 minutes
Cooking time: I hour I0 minutes
Serves 6

1.2kg boneless pork with some fat (like belly or shoulder), cut into large chunks

2-inch piece of cinnamon or cassia bark

½ tsp ground turmeric

I tbsp fine salt

100ml Goan/coconut vinegar

4 fresh green chillies, halved lengthways

2 tbsp vegetable, sunflower or rapeseed oil

2-3 large onions, finely chopped

½ tsp fine salt

300ml reserved pork cooking liquid

30g tamarind pulp or 2 tsp tamarind paste or I tsp tamarind concentrate

I tbsp jaggery, muscovado or fine brown sugar

For the sorpotel paste

2-inch piece of cinnamon or cassia bark

20 black peppercorns

I tsp cumin seeds

15 cloves

I whole large garlic bulb, individual cloves separated and peeled

2-inch piece (30g) of fresh ginger, unpeeled and roughly chopped

10 dried Kashmiri chillies, stalks removed, soaked in warm water for 5 minutes

150ml Goan/coconut vinegar

50ml cold water

A true Goan classic, pork sorpotel is often eaten at Christmas, weddings and special occasions. The dish originates from the Alentejo region of Portugal where it is made with lamb, goat, beef or pork. The recipe then travelled far and wide to the Portuguese colonies of Brazil and East Timor as well as Goa. Traditionally sorpotel includes offal – liver, heart, tongue and even blood – but my recipe omits all of the above to make it more universally pleasing! The meat is always parboiled in large chunks before being finely diced. It's a great recipe to make a few days in advance as the flavours are enhanced by resting in the fridge before reheating and serving.

1. Begin by placing the pork chunks in a large deep pan. Add the cinnamon or cassia bark, turmeric, fine salt, vinegar, 2 of the chillies and enough cold water to cover everything. Bring to the boil and simmer for 25 minutes.

2. Meanwhile, prepare the sorpotel paste. Begin by placing the cinnamon stick, black peppercorns, cumin seeds and cloves in a spice grinder. Grind to a fine powder and then add to a wet grinder along with the garlic cloves, ginger, soaked Kashmiri chillies, vinegar and cold water. Blitz to form a smooth paste and then set aside.

3. Strain the pork cooking liquid into a jug and set aside. Finely chop the pork meat and fat into half-inch cubes.

4. In a wide pan of medium depth, add half of the cubed pork and brown on a medium to high heat (as it contains fat, you won't need to add any oil). Stir intermittently so that it browns evenly. Remove with a slotted spoon and repeat with the remaining pork.

5. Setting the pork aside, add the oil, onions and salt to the same pan. Soften and lightly bronze the onion over the next 6 to 8 minutes.

6. Meanwhile, if using tamarind pulp, place it in a small bowl and cover with warm water. Leave it to soak for I0 minutes, then use your whole hand to break it up completely. Strain through a sieve into a bowl and use the back of a spoon to push through all the pulp. Discard the fibrous parts and seeds.

7. Add the sorpotel paste to the onions, mix well and stir while the paste cooks for 5 minutes. Add 300ml of the reserved pork cooking liquid and the tamarind pulp, paste or concentrate. Mix well, then return the pork to the pan.

8. Add the jaggery or sugar and finally the remaining 2 green chillies. Leave to simmer for a further 20 minutes with the lid on.

9. Taste to check whether the dish needs any extra sweetness or salt, adjusting the seasoning accordingly. If making ahead, store in the fridge once cooled completely.

10. Serve the sorpotel with steamed basmati rice and Allegra's Kachumber Salad (see page 76) or simply as it is with sliced tomatoes, cucumbers, red onions, yoghurt and quartered lemons or limes alongside.

Notes: Goan vinegar is also known as coconut vinegar and is a staple ingredient in Goan cuisine, made from the fermented sap of coconut flowers. You can easily purchase it online in the UK, as well as from suppliers including Biona Organic (www.biona.co.uk). Jaggery is made from sugar cane or date palms. It can be found at Asian grocers and online.

Potato Bhaji

Preparation time: 10-15 minutes
Cooking time: 25 minutes
Serves 4

600g potatoes

2 tbsp vegetable, sunflower or
rapeseed oil

Pinch of asafoetida powder

1 tsp brown or black mustard seeds

1 tsp cumin seeds

15 fresh or frozen curry leaves

1 medium white onion, finely chopped

7 garlic cloves, finely chopped

1 heaped tsp finely grated fresh ginger

1-2 fresh green chillies, diced
(deseeded for less heat)

½ tsp ground turmeric

400ml water

1 tsp fine salt

Fresh coriander leaves, to serve
(optional)

Nestled in the small, rural village of Batim in North Goa sits the Casa Menezes residence: a picturesque heritage homestay with tall, swaying palms, paddy fields, saltpans and a beautiful lake surrounding the village. Breakfasts are worth getting up for there. Each morning Goan potato bhaji was prepared for us by the staff of the homestay. We ate it with freshly baked warm *pao* or *sanna*, the Goan version of Indian *idli* (savoury rice cakes).

1. Cook the potatoes whole in their skins in boiling water for 15 to 20 minutes until soft. Check with a sharp knife and cook for a little longer if needed, then drain and set aside to cool before removing the skins and cutting into half-inch cubes.

2. Heat the oil in a wide pan of medium depth and when hot, add the asafoetida, mustard seeds and cumin seeds. These will immediately begin to pop so keep the heat low.

3. Add the curry leaves and white onion, mixing well. After 4 minutes, once the onion has softened, add the garlic and ginger. After another minute add the fresh green chilli and turmeric.

4. Return the softened potato to the pan along with the water. Use the back of a spoon to mash up some of the potato to help thicken the gravy.

5. Add the salt, check the seasoning is to your taste and simmer gently for a further 7 minutes before serving. Scatter with the fresh coriander if you like.

Pork with Kokum

Preparation time: 15 minutes
Cooking time: 1 hour (or 35 minutes
in pressure cooker, see notes on
page 9)
Serves 4-6

1.2kg pork, diced into 1 or 2 inch cubes

1 tsp fine salt

1 tsp sugar, or to taste

1 tsp ground turmeric

1 tsp freshly ground black pepper

1 large red onion, roughly chopped

15 garlic cloves, peeled

2 tsp finely grated fresh ginger

6 dried Kashmiri chillies, stalks removed
and broken in half

15 kokum (if dried, soak in warm
water for 10 minutes)

1 tbsp white vinegar

200ml water

30g tamarind pulp or 2 tsp tamarind
paste or 1 tsp tamarind concentrate

In Goa, this dish is often referred to as pork *solantulem*, *amsol* or *binda sol*. You may not have heard of kokum before, but it is available dried at most Asian grocers or online in the UK. Grown in India's Western Ghats in the states of Goa, Maharashtra, Karnataka and Kerala, kokum is a small red fruit from a plant of the mangosteen family that turns a deep purple as it ripens. Similar to tamarind, it brings a delicious sourness to dishes. This one is so simple, balanced, packed full of flavour and yet has very few ingredients. You can find recipes for this dish that add more spices – cloves, cinnamon, cumin and coriander – but this is the way it was prepared for me on a recent trip to Goa and I feel it is close to how the Portuguese would have liked to prepare it, with just a few spices and the vinegar.

1. Place the pork in a large mixing bowl and add all the ingredients except the water and tamarind. Mix well, cover and set aside to marinate for 30 minutes.

2. Heat a deep casserole pan or pressure cooker and add the contents of the mixing bowl. You don't need to add any oil here as the pork will release enough fat. Stir for a few minutes before adding the water.

3. Simmer on a medium to low heat with the lid on for 30 minutes, stirring intermittently. In a pressure cooker it will only need to cook for 20 minutes.

4. Meanwhile, if using tamarind pulp, place it in a small bowl and cover with warm water. Leave it to soak for 10 minutes, then use your whole hand to break it up completely. Strain through a sieve into a bowl and use the back of a spoon to push through all the pulp. Discard the fibrous parts and seeds.

5. Add the prepared tamarind pulp, paste or concentrate to the pork and stir in. Place the lid back on the pan and leave to cook for a further 15 minutes. If you're using a pressure cooker, you only need to cook on the hob for 5 minutes at this stage.

6. To reduce the liquid in the pan, remove the lid and cook uncovered for a final 10 minutes. This dish is all about the balance of sour and salty flavours, so taste before serving and adjust the seasoning if required. Enjoy with the Parsi 'Brown' Rice on page 186.

Notes: You can cook this dish in the oven for 1 hour at 200°C/180°C fan/400°F/ Gas 6 instead of on the hob – just give it a good stir halfway through and if it is looking too dry, add a little water to loosen the gravy.

Tamarind pulp, as opposed to paste or concentrate, is available at Asian grocery stores and some large supermarkets, usually found in block form wrapped in cellophane. It stores in the fridge for months. I tend to buy it in this form but tamarind paste is equally good. If you buy tamarind concentrate, use with caution as it's much stronger in flavour.

Prawn Balchão

Preparation time: 10 minutes
Cooking time: 50 minutes
Serves 4-6

1kg medium or large prawns, cleaned and deveined

¼ tsp ground turmeric

2 tsp fine salt

6 tbsp coconut oil or vegetable oil

1 large white onion, finely chopped

4 garlic cloves, finely chopped

3 large tomatoes, finely chopped or blitzed to a purée

1 tbsp fine brown or caster sugar, or to taste

For the paste

5 dried Kashmiri chillies, seeds and stems removed

6 cloves

1 tsp cumin seeds

1 tsp black peppercorns

1 tsp black or brown mustard seeds

2-inch piece of cinnamon or cassia bark

1.5-inch piece (23g) of ginger, chopped

6 garlic cloves, roughly chopped

100ml apple cider vinegar

Traditionally, balchão was regarded as a Goan Portuguese pickle that was eaten during the monsoon months when fisherman did not go out to sea to fish. Due to the use of vinegar, it would last for many months if stored correctly in a sealed jar. Today it is so popular that it is often served as a dish that is eaten immediately. An authentic recipe would include powdered dried shrimp, in addition to fresh prawns, but as they are hard to source outside of Goa, they are often left out completely. Toddy vinegar is often used too, but outside of Goa a fruit vinegar like apple cider vinegar will work well. No water is added to this recipe if you are going to pickle it, but if you are going to eat it immediately then you can add a little water to loosen the paste.

1. Place the prawns in a bowl with the turmeric and 1 teaspoon of the salt. Leave to rest while you continue with the next steps.

2. To make the paste, first toast the chillies and spices in a dry pan for 1 to 2 minutes to awaken their aromas, then remove and blitz in a spice grinder to make a masala.

3. Blitz the ginger and garlic in a wet grinder, then add the masala and vinegar. Blitz again to form a smooth paste.

4. In a wide frying pan of medium depth, heat two tablespoons of the oil and fry the prawns in batches for around 3 to 4 minutes on each side until lightly bronzed. Set aside on kitchen paper and repeat, adding more oil if required, until all the prawns are sealed.

5. Using the same pan, heat the remaining oil and then add the onion and remaining salt. Allow to soften and become lightly bronzed, which will take 6 to 8 minutes.

6. Add the garlic, then after another minute add the tomatoes and sugar and allow to soften over the next 3 to 4 minutes.

7. Add the paste to the pan and mix well before returning the prawns to the pan. Fold the prawns into the paste so that they are completely coated. Keep the heat low and simmer for 3 to 4 minutes with a lid on the pan. You will notice some oil rising to the surface, which is the signal that the dish is ready.

8. If you are going to pickle the prawns, cook them for a few minutes longer. Transfer the balchão into a sterilised jar and allow to cool before storing. It will keep in a cool pantry or fridge for a few months.

9. If you are going to eat it immediately, you can add a little water to loosen the paste and then the balchão is ready to eat.

Rissois de Camarão

Preparation time: 30 minutes
Cooking time: 30 minutes
Makes 16

This very typical Goan Portuguese appetiser is as much loved in Goa as it is in Portugal. It literally translates to 'patties of prawns' which are shaped into half-moons, then dipped in egg wash and breadcrumbed before being fried until crisp. The prawn filling includes a white sauce, also known as béchamel, with only a hint of spice in the form of nutmeg and black pepper. I also like to add chilli flakes to the filling but whether you use chilli or not is totally up to you.

For the filling

2 tbsp butter or olive oil

½ onion, finely chopped

1 tsp fine salt

3 garlic cloves, roughly chopped

150g prawns, peeled, deveined and roughly chopped

½ tsp freshly ground black pepper

1 tsp chilli flakes (optional)

For the béchamel

1 tbsp butter

1 tbsp plain flour

120ml milk

1 heaped tbsp grated cheddar cheese

¼ tsp nutmeg

For the pastry and coating

2 tbsp butter

½ tsp salt

250ml water

250g plain flour

1 egg, whisked

120g fine or panko breadcrumbs

Vegetable or sunflower oil, enough for shallow frying or deep frying if you prefer

1. Begin by making the filling. Heat the butter or oil in a frying pan, add the onion and salt and cook for 4 to 5 minutes so that the onion remains translucent.

2. Add the garlic and cook for another minute before adding the prawns. Allow them to turn pink before adding the black pepper, and chilli flakes if using. Stir for 3 minutes and then remove this mixture from the pan and place in a bowl.

3. Use the same pan to make the béchamel. Melt the butter and then add the flour, stirring to combine until you have a smooth paste. Cook this for a minute, moving it around to avoid catching on the bottom of the pan, then gradually add the milk while stirring or whisking constantly. Stir in the cheese and nutmeg, along with an extra splash of milk if needed to adjust the consistency. Keep whisking until a smooth sauce is formed.

4. Add the prawn mixture to the sauce and keep the pan on the heat for a couple of minutes, allowing all the ingredients to combine. Turn the filling out into a bowl and then clean the pan before using it again for a third time.

5. While it might seem strange, you are going to make the pastry in the pan. Melt the butter and then add the salt, water and flour. Use a spatula to help it all combine and then immediately turn off the heat.

6. Sprinkle a little flour onto a clean surface and turn out the warm pastry dough from the pan. Immediately break off a piece of dough the size of a golf ball and roll out into a 3mm thick disc approximately 4 inches in diameter while it is still warm.

7. Place a teaspoon of the prawn filling just off-centre on the disc of dough, then fold the dough up and over so that the filling is completely encased in pastry. Use the rim of a glass or cup to apply pressure around the edge where the dough meets, sealing the patty and creating a half-moon shape.

(Continued overleaf)

Rissois de Camarão (Continued)

8. Set aside and repeat, using up the rest of the dough and prawn mixture. You could, if you prefer, roll out all the rounds of dough first, before adding the filling and sealing them. I personally favour this method of making each patty in turn, for uniformity and to ensure the patties are properly closed. Be careful not to overfill the patties.

9. You can now freeze the patties at this stage (once cooled) if you're making them in advance. Place in the freezer on a plate or tray, allow them to harden and then store in resealable bags.

10. If you want to eat the patties immediately, whisk the egg with a tablespoon of water in one shallow bowl and place the breadcrumbs in another.

11. Using one hand, dip the patty into the egg wash and then place in the bowl of breadcrumbs. Use your other (dry) hand to coat the patty with the breadcrumbs, then place it on a clean plate ready for frying. Repeat with all the patties. They can be kept in the fridge for up to 2 hours at this stage if you want to get ahead before frying.

12. Heat the oil in a small pan and sprinkle a few breadcrumbs in the oil. If they immediately sizzle, the oil is the right temperature. Gently lower the patties into the oil in batches. Shallow or deep fry until bronzed on both sides – this should take around 2 minutes in total. Remove the patties with a slotted spoon and place on kitchen paper, ready to eat.

Notes: You can add half a teaspoon of smoked paprika or a few drops of your favourite hot sauce to the filling if you wish. To cook from frozen, bring the patties out of the freezer 30 minutes before you want to fry them, then continue with the recipe above from Step 10. For a vegetarian alternative, try replacing the prawns with paneer or mushrooms. After frying, allow the oil to cool and then strain and decant into a clean, empty bottle to be reused.

Pao

Preparation time: 10 minutes, plus 1 hour 45 minutes proving
Cooking time: 20 minutes, plus 30 minutes resting
Makes 9 rolls

500g plain flour
2 tsp easy bake/instant yeast
1 tsp white caster sugar
1 tsp fine salt
100ml warm (not hot) milk
170ml lukewarm water
60g + 1 tbsp melted butter
1 egg, whisked or 20ml milk

The Portuguese introduced bread leavened with yeast to India. Goan pao, or *pav* as they are also referred to, are simply leavened bread rolls: soft, fluffy and perfect for scooping up a curry, dipping into hot soup or dal. They're fun to make and require very few ingredients, although the proving does take time so plan in advance when you want to give these a try. The results are always very pleasing. In Goa, fresh batches are made each day for breakfast.

1. Place the flour, yeast, sugar and salt in a large mixing bowl and mix well.

2. Slowly add a little of the milk and water into the flour along with the 60g of melted butter. Use one hand to hold the bowl still and the other to mix the ingredients together.

3. Gradually add more of the liquids and continue to form a dough. When it comes together, turn the dough out onto a clean work surface, scattering over a little flour if required to stop it sticking, and knead for a good 6 to 8 minutes, folding over and stretching to introduce air into the dough.

4. Place the kneaded dough in an oiled bowl and cover with a damp cloth or clingfilm. Leave in a warm place for the dough to double in size over the next hour (see notes).

5. Once proved, lightly punch the air out of the dough and then turn onto a work surface. Knead again for 3 to 4 minutes and then divide the dough into 9 equal balls. Place them on an oiled or lightly floured baking tray, half an inch apart. Cover this tray with the same damp cloth or clingfilm and return to the warm place for a further 45 minutes, by which time the dough balls will have risen and be pressing firmly against one another.

6. Heat the oven to 220°C/200°C fan/425°F/Gas 7. Gently brush the tops of the proved rolls with the whisked egg or milk to give them a lovely glazed crust.

7. Bake for 20 minutes in the preheated oven. Remove and lightly brush the remaining tablespoon of melted butter over the rolls to give them extra shine.

8. Cover with a cloth and leave at room temperature for 30 minutes before serving. This makes them extra soft. They are best eaten fresh or within two days at most.

Notes: If you prefer to use active dry yeast, you need to activate it before use with a teaspoon of sugar and a little warm (not hot!) water. Combine in a small bowl and leave for 10 minutes.

When proving dough, I always pop the oven on a low heat for 5 minutes and then turn it off completely, keeping the oven door slightly ajar and the light switched on. I then place the covered bowl of dough in the warm oven to prove until it rises. If you live in a warm climate, simply leave the covered dough to one side and it will prove at room temperature.

Stuffed Small Aubergines
with Recheado Masala

Preparation time: 35 minutes
Cooking time: 15-20 minutes
Serves 4

8 small oval-shaped aubergines

1 tbsp fine salt

1 heaped tsp recheado masala per
aubergine (see page 144)

2 tbsp vegetable, sunflower or
rapeseed oil

For this recipe, you want to look out for the aubergines that look like large eggs (this is how they originally got their alternative name of eggplant). Before starting this dish, you'll need to make the recheado masala on page 144 which takes no longer than 15 minutes. Typically, recheado is used as a coating for fish when fried but it also works really well as a stuffing for vegetables. Okra, also known as lady's fingers, are equally tasty prepared in this way.

1. Begin by making two slits in the shape of a cross three quarters of the way down the aubergine, without cutting all the way through so that they stay intact.

2. Next, generously salt the aubergines in the shallow cross you have just created. Place the aubergines in a sieve over a bowl and leave to stand for 30 minutes. Salting draws out the moisture and means you will require less oil when cooking.

3. After 30 minutes, discard the water which will have gathered in the bowl under the sieve, then wash the aubergines to remove the salt and pat dry.

4. Use a teaspoon to stuff the recheado masala into the crosses in each aubergine.

5. Heat a frying pan and add the oil. When hot, add the aubergines and allow them to soften on a medium heat. Place a lid on the pan and turn the aubergines at intervals once they have softened on each side. This process will take around 15 minutes.

6. When cooked through, serve the stuffed aubergines on a plate alongside some Goan Pao (see page 140) or Arroz Pulao (see page 114).

Notes: If you cannot find small oval aubergines you can use regular ones but cut them in half lengthways, then after salting slather the masala over the cut sides of the aubergines rather than stuffing them. They can then be cooked in a frying pan, in the oven or even on a barbecue until softened.

Recheado Masala

Preparation time: 5 minutes
Cooking time: 10 minutes
Makes 1 large jar

1 medium red onion

20 dried Kashmiri chillies (deseeded for less heat)

12 garlic cloves

8 cloves

2-inch piece of cinnamon or cassia bark

1 tsp black peppercorns

1 tsp cumin seeds

¼ tsp ground turmeric

1 tsp fine salt

3 tsp caster or light brown sugar

4 tbsp red wine vinegar

1 tbsp vegetable, sunflower or rapeseed oil

Recheado means 'stuffed' in Portuguese and it is this masala paste that is found all over the state of Goa. It's so versatile and can be used to stuff or coat a wide range of seafood as well as vegetables such as small oval aubergines (see page 142), okra and even bitter melon (*karela*). As the Portuguese had long sea voyages to endure, a masala paste that could preserve foods thanks to the inclusion of vinegar would probably have been a welcome addition to their culinary repertoire on board. In Goa, the local vinegar is used along with a splash of cashew *feni* (see notes). Outside Goa, red wine vinegar is a good substitute.

1. If you have a gas hob, place the whole onion, with the skin on, into the flame to char on all sides. Use tongs to turn it over regularly. Once cooled slightly, remove the skin and then roughly slice. If you do not have a gas hob, peel and finely slice the onion, then place in a dry frying pan on a medium heat and cook without oil for a few minutes until it softens and the raw smell vanishes.

2. Now place all the ingredients, including the onion, in a wet grinder and blitz until a smooth paste forms. If it is quite thick, or needs to be smoother, add an extra splash of vinegar and blitz again. Taste and add more salt or sugar as required.

3. Store the masala paste in a sterilised and sealed glass jar in the fridge. It will keep for up to 6 months.

Notes: Cashew *feni*, a colourless spirit distilled from the juice of fermented cashew apples, is exclusively produced in Goa.

Banana and Cinnamon Fritters

Preparation time: 5 minutes
Cooking time: 15 minutes
Makes 20

2 medium or large bananas, ideally overripe

1-2 tsp jaggery, light brown sugar or icing sugar, to taste

½ tsp vanilla extract

¼ tsp ground cinnamon

I egg

225g plain flour

200ml milk

I tbsp butter, ghee or sunflower, vegetable or rapeseed oil

In the local Goan language of Konkani, these fritters are known as *filos*. They are very similar to a British drop scone and the perfect teatime treat, as well as a helpful recipe for using up overripe bananas! I like to add a sprinkling of cinnamon to mine, but that is optional.

1. In a mixing bowl, use a fork to break up the bananas and mash them to a smooth paste.

2. Add the jaggery or sugar, vanilla essence, cinnamon and egg. Mix well.

3. Sift the flour into the bowl and stir until everything is combined.

4. Add the milk and mix to a smooth pancake batter. If you find it is still a little thick at this stage, simply add a dash more milk. Taste the batter to see if it needs a little more cinnamon or sugar, according to your preference.

5. Melt the butter or heat the oil in a frying pan and then pour in a little pancake batter to form a small pancake. Cook for 1 to 2 minutes, then carefully flip and cook for another 1 to 2 minutes on the other side.

6. Once nicely bronzed, remove from the pan and continue with the remaining batter, cooking in batches depending on the size of your pan. Enjoy while they are still hot.

Tibetan Nepalese

In the northeast reaches of India, amidst the Himalayas, sits the multiethnic and multilingual state of Sikkim and further south, the picturesque hill station of Darjeeling in West Bengal. Dramatic landscapes of glaciers and alpine meadows give this whole region a unique biodiversity and charm. As a result of this area's geography – Sikkim borders Tibet, Nepal, Bhutan and West Bengal – a fusion of traditions and flavours has developed over the years within its culturally diverse populations. The official languages of Sikkim are English, Nepali, Sikkimese and Lepcha; the Lepchas are an indigenous group of people from the Himalayas straddling Nepal and India who are thought to have Mongolian ancestry. Additional languages spoken there include Gurung, Limbu, Magar, Newari, Rai, Sherpa and Tamang. With such diversity across this region, it's easy to see how each group has brought their own customs and habits to the table, fusing them to result in the highly distinctive and comforting Tibetan Nepalese cuisine.

From the 1800s, the British in India retreated to the cool mountain town of Darjeeling during the hot summer months, escaping from the sweltering heat of Calcutta. It was seen as the perfect terrain, altitude and climate in which to establish tea plantations that have since put Darjeeling on the map as one of the most celebrated tea-growing regions of the world.

Owing to the cold, harsh winters when fresh vegetables are harder to source in Sikkim and West Bengal, fermented food is prepared in advance over the summer months. The most famous dish is *gundruk*, which has Nepali origins and is made with leafy mustard greens and radish or cabbage leaves that are shredded and fermented in an airtight container for five days. It is then dried on bamboo mats under the hot sun for a few days to crisp up before being stored, ready to be eaten over the winter months, often in a piping hot broth to provide warmth and sustenance.

The street food of the region reflects the culinary influences of its people too; *sel roti*, another Nepalese export, is a large ring-shaped doughnut made of rice flour, sugar, oil or ghee and sweet-smelling aromatic spices such as cinnamon, cardamom or cloves – the perfect teatime snack to enjoy with Darjeeling tea. On a more savoury note, the momo is undoubtedly the most loved snack of the region: a dumpling with many meat and vegetarian fillings to choose from. Similarly, their *tingmo* (steamed buns) make an excellent accompaniment to many of the stews and curries throughout this book.

Sichuan peppercorns, known as *yerma* in Tibet, appear in several dishes within this chapter, creating an addictively numbing sensation on the tongue. If you haven't used them before, I highly encourage you to seek them out – they are easy to find online and in Asian grocery stores. They really announce their presence so use them sparingly!

Nepali Mixed Lentil Stew

Preparation time: 15 minutes
Cooking time: 45 minutes
Serves 6

100g red split lentils

100g yellow moong/mung lentils

900ml cold water

2 tbsp vegetable, sunflower or rapeseed oil

1 tsp cumin seeds

½ tsp ajwain/carom seeds

¼ tsp fenugreek seeds

¼ tsp asafoetida powder (optional)

2 dried whole red chillies

1 large onion, finely chopped

1 tsp fine salt

1 heaped tsp finely grated garlic

1 heaped tsp finely grated fresh ginger

1 tsp ground turmeric

1 tsp ground coriander

½ tsp ground cumin

½ tsp Kashmiri chilli powder (optional)

3 large tomatoes, diced

2 tbsp finely chopped fresh coriander leaves and stalks

2 x 400g jars or tins of red kidney beans, black-eyed beans, chickpeas, green lentils, butter beans or white beans, drained and rinsed

300ml water

Juice of ½ a lemon

Known as *kwati* – kwa meaning hot and ti meaning soup or broth in Newari – this mixed lentil stew originated in Nepal, where the Newars – the inhabitants of the Kathmandu valley – would eat it for nourishment and strength as they farmed the land. It is also hugely popular across the northeastern part of India, particularly in Darjeeling. Traditionally, *kwati* is made with nine different beans and lentils that are soaked for 24 hours before being drained and covered with a damp cloth, which is lightly sprinkled with water over the following 48 hours so that the beans begin to germinate. My version is far less labour intensive thanks to jarred or tinned beans and quick-cooking lentils. Adding fenugreek seeds, asafoetida and ajwain seeds helps to prevent gas and bloating which can otherwise result from eating so many pulses.

1. Place the lentils in a bowl and cover with water. Give them a good wash, using your hand to stir thoroughly, then drain and place in a large, deep pan. Cover with the 900ml of fresh cold water.

2. Bring to the boil and simmer for 15 to 20 minutes. While it cooks, skim off and discard any scum or froth that rises to the surface.

3. To check the lentils have cooked, remove some with a teaspoon and squeeze between your thumb and forefinger. They should give easily and feel soft when they are done so if the lentils still have some bite, cook for a little longer and add more water if needed.

4. In a separate pan, heat the oil and then add the cumin, ajwain and fenugreek seeds along with the asafoetida (if using) and dried chillies. Stir for 10 seconds before adding the onion and salt.

5. Fry the onion for 6 to 7 minutes until lightly bronzed and then add the garlic and ginger. After another minute, add the ground turmeric, coriander, cumin and Kashmiri chilli powder. Mix well before adding the tomatoes.

6. Let the tomatoes break down and release their juices over the next 4 to 5 minutes. Add 1 tablespoon of the fresh coriander and then stir in the beans and/or pulses of your choice.

7. Pour the cooked lentils into the spiced tomato base, add the extra water and stir thoroughly to mix all the ingredients together.

8. Simmer the stew for 10 minutes and then taste to check the seasoning, adding more salt if required. Finally, stir in the remaining fresh coriander and lemon juice to serve.

Notes: This stew freezes well and is great eaten over a few days. Simply top up with a little water if the consistency becomes too thick when reheating.

Vegetable Thukpa

Preparation time: 15 minutes
Cooking time: 20 minutes
Serves 4

2 tbsp vegetable, sunflower or
rapeseed oil

1 onion, finely sliced

1 tsp fine salt

1-inch piece (15g) of fresh ginger,
peeled and cut into thin batons

6 spring onions, finely sliced

2 garlic cloves, finely chopped or grated

1 large carrot, cut into thin 1 or 2 inch
batons

¼ white or savoy cabbage, finely sliced

1-2 fresh chillies, halved lengthways
(deseed for less heat)

Handful of fresh coriander stems, finely
chopped

½ tsp freshly ground black pepper

Juice of ½ a lemon

1 tbsp light soy sauce

600ml vegetable stock

1 tsp honey

3 nests of egg noodles

Handful of fresh coriander leaves, finely
chopped, to serve

The weather can be chilling in the foothills of the Himalayas, so a warming noodle soup or stew is one way of gaining nourishment and warmth. Originating in Tibet, when the Dalai Lama sought refuge in India in 1959, the tradition of cooking this dish spread far and wide and it continues to be hugely popular in Darjeeling, Sikkim and Arunachal Pradesh. I included a recipe for chicken thukpa in my first cookbook, *Chilli & Mint*, so here is a deliciously simple vegetable version. Perfect for chilly days.

1. Heat the oil in a large pan and then add the onion and salt. Keep it moving around the pan for 3 minutes before adding the ginger batons, three quarters of the spring onions and the garlic.
2. After a minute, add the carrot and cabbage. Fold them into the contents of the pan, then add the fresh chillies, coriander stems, black pepper, lemon juice and soy sauce, followed by the vegetable stock. Simmer for 8 minutes and then add the honey.
3. Meanwhile, cook the egg noodles in a separate pan according to the packet instructions (they usually take around 6 to 8 minutes).
4. If you need to top up the soup with more liquid, ladle some of the starchy cooking water from the noodle pan into the soup pan.
5. When the noodles are cooked, drain them and divide between serving bowls. Ladle the soup over the noodles, then scatter with the fresh coriander leaves and reserved spring onions.

Notes: I like to add a dollop of hot sauce to this thukpa – see the recipe on page 176. This is great as a light meal or starter but if you want to make it heartier and more filling, you could add protein such as tofu.

Chicken Curry Himalayan Style

Preparation time: 15 minutes
Cooking time: 30 minutes
Makes 4-6

For the paste

1 tsp cumin seeds

4 dried whole red chillies

2-inch piece (30g) of fresh ginger, peeled or unpeeled and roughly chopped

6 garlic cloves, peeled

3 tbsp water

For the curry

2 tbsp vegetable, sunflower or rapeseed oil

1 tsp cumin seeds

2 dried whole chillies

1-2 fresh green chillies, slit lengthways

1 large onion, finely diced

1 tsp fine salt

½ tsp ground turmeric

1 tsp ground coriander

1kg boneless chicken thighs, cut into bite-size pieces

2 large tomatoes, finely diced

150ml water

1 tbsp plain flour or cornflour

3 tbsp cold water

1 tsp garam masala

2 tbsp finely chopped fresh coriander leaves

The foothills of the Himalayas in India are a melting pot of people from Tibet, Nepal, Bhutan and Sikkim, all living side by side but each with their own styles and nuances of cooking. This simple curry is commonly found in the region and has its roots in Nepali cuisine.

1. Place the paste ingredients in a wet grinder and blitz to form a smooth paste. Add a splash more water if required to loosen the consistency.

2. Heat the oil in a large, wide pan with a lid. Add the cumin seeds and both types of chillies. Move them around for 20 seconds and then add the onion and salt.

3. Allow the onion to lightly bronze, which will take around 6 to 8 minutes, then add the ground turmeric and coriander. Stir well and then add the paste. Simmer gently for 3 minutes before adding the chicken.

4. Coat the chicken in the spices and then add the diced tomatoes. Stir intermittently for the next 5 minutes, making sure the chicken does not catch on the bottom of the pan.

5. Add the water and simmer for 15 minutes with a lid on the pan. The water should have reduced a little after this time and the gravy will have become thicker. If it needs a little help to thicken, make a slurry by mixing the plain flour or cornflour with the cold water in a small bowl. Add this to the pan while stirring the curry and it will thicken on heating.

6. Finally, add the garam masala and mix well, followed by the fresh coriander leaves. Serve with basmati rice.

Bamboo Shoot and Potato Curry

Preparation time: 15 minutes
Cooking time: 30 minutes
Serves 4-6

This recipe is a favourite in the northeast Indian state of Sikkim, a region that borders Tibet, Bhutan and Nepal. Typically, it's made with fresh bamboo shoots, but is also great with tinned bamboo, which is easy to get hold of.

2 tbsp vegetable, sunflower or rapeseed oil

1 tsp panch phoron (Bengali five spice)

1 medium onion, finely sliced

1 tsp fine salt

1 heaped tsp finely grated garlic

1 heaped tsp finely grated fresh ginger

2 fresh chillies, halved lengthways

2 medium tomatoes (approx. 150g), roughly chopped

2 medium potatoes (approx. 350g), cut into 1-inch cubes

½ tsp Kashmiri chilli powder

1 tsp ground turmeric

1 tsp ground cumin

1 tsp ground coriander

1 tsp mango powder (amchoor)

700ml water

1 x 400g jar or tin of black-eyed beans

440g bamboo shoots

1. Heat the oil in a wide, deep pan with a lid. Add the panch phoron (Bengali five spice) and then the sliced onion and salt.

2. Allow the onion to soften and lightly bronze over the next 4 to 5 minutes before adding the grated garlic and ginger along with the fresh chillies.

3. After a minute, add the chopped tomatoes followed by the cubed potatoes. Coat the potatoes in the contents of the pan and simmer gently, turning them every so often.

4. Add the ground spices, including the mango powder, and mix well. After a couple of minutes, add the water and place a lid on the pan. Cook for 15 minutes, allowing the potato to soften completely.

5. Add the black-eyed beans and bamboo shoots to the curry, folding them in. Simmer on a medium heat for a further 5 minutes.

6. This can be eaten on its own for a very comforting and filling vegan meal.

Notes: Panch phoron is a blend of five spices from Bengal which includes equal parts black or brown mustard seeds, nigella seeds, cumin seeds, fennel seeds and fenugreek. You can find it in some supermarkets but otherwise look for panch phoron in Asian grocers or online (see page 244 for suppliers). The black-eyed beans in this dish can be replaced with black, white or cannellini beans if you prefer.

Shaptak

Preparation time: 15 minutes
Cooking time: 12-15 minutes
Serves 4

3 tbsp sunflower, vegetable or
rapeseed oil

2 dried whole red chillies, broken in
half

2 red onions, quartered and separated
into petals

2 garlic cloves, finely chopped or grated

1-inch piece (15g) of fresh ginger, finely
chopped or grated

2 celery sticks, chopped into thin half-
moons

¼ bell pepper, cut into 2 inch-cubes

450g boneless pork, sirloin/flank steak,
lamb neck, chicken thighs or mixed
mushrooms, very thinly sliced into
2-inch strips

1 tsp Sichuan peppercorns, crushed
(see notes)

2 tbsp light soy sauce

300ml chicken, beef, lamb or vegetable
stock (½ a cube)

1 tbsp plain flour or cornflour

3 tbsp cold water

2 spring onions, green parts only, finely
sliced

This quick and easy Tibetan stir-fry is traditionally eaten alongside *tingmo*, the Tibetan steamed buns on page 160. Traditionally the protein would be yak meat, which is common across the Himalayan ranges, but this dish works equally well with beef, chicken, lamb, pork or mushrooms. Bell pepper or celery is usually added to complete the dish.

1. Heat the oil in a skillet or wok and when hot, add the dried chillies and onion petals. Stir fry for 2 minutes before adding the garlic, ginger, celery and bell pepper.

2. Cook for another 2 minutes and then add the meat or mushrooms of your choice along with the Sichuan peppercorns. Stir fry over a high heat for 4 to 5 minutes.

3. Add the soy sauce and then the stock to the stir fry. In a small bowl, mix the flour or cornflour with the cold water to make a smooth paste, then stir this into the stock which will thicken as it heats.

4. Cook for another couple of minutes and if you want the stock to reduce for an even thicker sauce, cook for a few minutes longer.

5. Finally, add the spring onions and cook for a final minute, then serve immediately with some freshly made *tingmo* or noodles.

Notes: If you do not have Sichuan peppercorns, you can substitute them with a teaspoon of Chinese five spice, crushed black peppercorns or ground white pepper. I highly recommend Sichuan peppercorns though, which are easy to source online.

Colourful Tibetan Steamed Buns

Preparation time: 30 minutes, plus 90 minutes proving
Cooking time: 25-30 minutes
Makes 10 small or 5 large buns

1 tsp easy bake/instant yeast or active dry yeast

1 tsp caster sugar

20ml warm water

250g white plain flour

140ml warm water

1 tsp fine salt

1 tbsp vegetable or sunflower oil

Optional

½ tsp ground turmeric (for yellow dough)

25ml beetroot juice (for pink dough – reduce water by 25ml)

4 spring onions, dark green parts only, finely sliced

Known as *tingmo*, these soft and airy Tibetan steamed buns can be found in the northern reaches of India (as well as in Tibet) where Tibetan culture thrives. They require very few ingredients and are very easy to make. Traditionally, they are plain with no additional flavours or colours but ingredients such as turmeric, Sichuan peppercorns, spring onions and beetroot juice can be introduced to make them even more delectable. When it comes to shaping the buns, you can get as creative as you like, although I would suggest keeping it simple to begin with. *Tingmo* are best eaten immediately along with the Himalayan Hot Sauce on page 176 or Shaptak on page 158. If you make them in advance and freeze them, simply steam from frozen for a few minutes longer to make them soft and fluffy.

To make the dough

1. If you are using easy bake/instant yeast, skip this step. If you are using active dry yeast, place it in a small bowl along with the caster sugar and add the 20ml of warm water. Mix well, then cover and set aside for 10 minutes to allow it to activate. Small bubbles will come to the surface, and it will begin to look frothy.

2. You can make the dough by hand in a large bowl, or in a stand mixer. Sift the flour into the bowl or mixer and add the salt. Stir well, then pour in the activated yeast or add the easy bake/instant yeast and use a chopstick to mix in a circular motion.

3. For yellow buns, add the turmeric at this stage. For pink buns, add the beetroot juice and reduce the quantity of water in the next step by 25ml. I often like to do a plain batch then follow it up with a batch of turmeric or beetroot.

4. Gradually add the 140ml of warm water as you mix the ingredients gently, allowing the flour to bind and form a dough ball. If you feel it needs a little more water, add in very small amounts. If the dough feels too wet, add a little more flour.

5. If you are making the dough by hand, lift it out once it has come together and knead on a clean surface for 10 minutes until it feels very soft and bounces back slightly when you poke it with your finger. In a stand mixer, use the dough hook attachment on a low speed (2 works well on my KitchenAid) for 5 to 7 minutes.

6. Return the dough to the bowl, rub some neutral oil on your hands and pat the dough all over to stop it drying out. Cover the bowl with clingfilm or a clean, damp tea towel and then leave the dough in a warm place to double in size for 1 hour 30 minutes (see notes).

(Continued overleaf...)

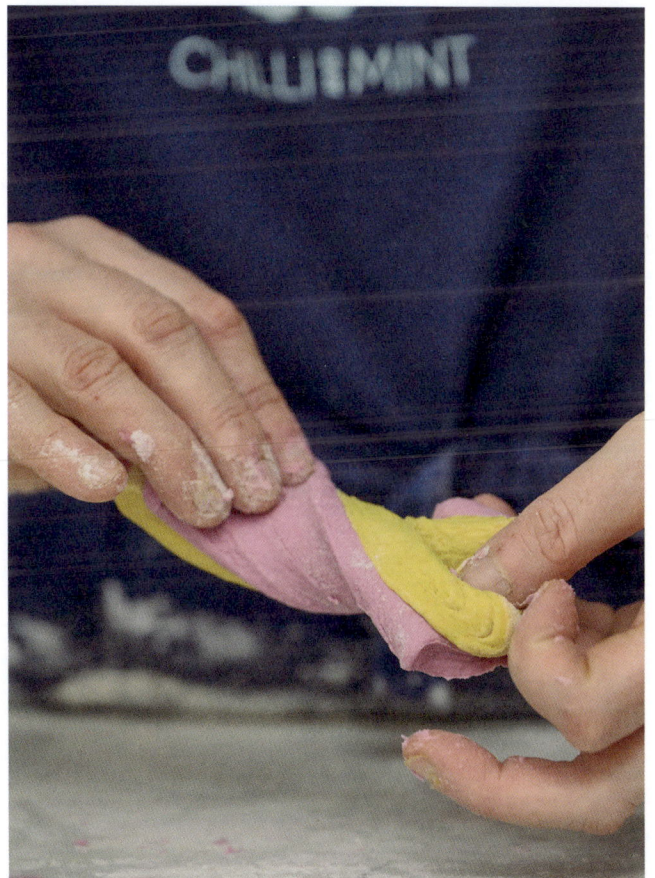

Colourful Tibetan Steamed Buns (Continued)

To make and steam the buns

1. If you are using a bamboo steamer, cut out rounds of baking paper for the individual buns to sit on, or one large round with little holes in to allow the steam through. Place these at the bottom of your steamer trays. If you are using a metal steamer, lightly the oil the bottom of your steam trays with neutral oil.

2. After 90 minutes, turn out the proved dough onto a clean surface and knead for a couple of minutes. Sprinkle a little more flour over the work surface if the dough feels sticky. Roll the dough into a large rectangle. For plain buns, skip the next step.

3. If you would like to make spring onion buns, drizzle a little oil over the rectangle of dough and then sprinkle with the sliced spring onions, ensuring they are evenly spread out.

4. Carefully fold the filled or plain dough rectangle up from the bottom to the width of a ruler, then fold again and again until you get to the top.

5. Use a sharp knife to cut the dough into 20 small pieces or 10 larger ones, aiming to make them all equal in size.

6. Place one of the dough pieces on top of another and press down to attach them. Gently pull the dough at each end to lengthen it, then twist it once or twice and fold the ends underneath to secure them and create a ball. Place the bun into your steamer and repeat with the remaining dough pieces.

7. At this stage, you can freeze the buns if you are making them ahead of time. Place them on a large baking tray, freeze and then transfer them to a resealable bag and store in the freezer until you are ready to cook and eat them.

8. If you are eating the buns immediately, pour water into the bottom of your steamer and bring to the boil. It is important that no water touches the buns at any stage so don't fill up your pan too much.

9. Steam the buns for 20 minutes. For frozen buns, steam for 25 minutes. After this time, turn off the heat and leave the lid on the pan for a couple of minutes.

10. Once rested, the buns are ready to eat. They are very tasty with Himalayan Hot Sauce (page 176), Sichuan Chilli Sauce (page 44) or soy sauce for dipping.

Notes: When proving dough, I always pop the oven on a low heat for 5 minutes and then turn it off completely, keeping the oven door slightly ajar and the light switched on. I then place the covered bowl of dough in the warm oven to prove until it rises. If you live in a warm climate, simply leave the covered dough to one side and it will prove at room temperature.

When making these buns, I like to make two or even three batches of the dough so you can mix and match the colours, using yellow and pink pieces in combination with the plain or spring onion dough for fun variations and colour combinations.

Phingsha – Chicken with Glass Noodles

Preparation time: 45 minutes
Cooking time: 25 minutes
Serves 4-6

10g dried wood ear mushrooms, or fresh shiitake mushrooms

150g glass noodles

2 tbsp vegetable, sunflower or rapeseed oil

2 dried whole chillies, broken into pieces

1-2 fresh green chillies, halved lengthways (optional)

2 medium white onion, thinly sliced

1 heaped tsp finely grated garlic

1 heaped tsp finely grated fresh ginger

4 large tomatoes, roughly chopped

200g potatoes, diced into 1-inch cubes

1 tsp Sichuan peppercorns, crushed

400g boneless chicken thighs, cut into small bite-size cubes or strips

½ tsp ground white pepper

½ tsp ground turmeric

1 tsp fine salt

2 tbsp light soy sauce

1 chicken or vegetable stock cube

2 handfuls of spinach or bok choy (optional)

For the topping

2 tbsp vegetable, sunflower or rapeseed oil

2 banana shallots, finely sliced

2 spring onions, finely sliced

Phingsha is a Himalayan dish popular in Darjeeling, Kalimpong and Sikkim, areas which are an ethnic melting pot of tribes with Tibetan and Nepalese ancestry. Phing are glass noodles – also called bean thread or cellophane noodles – and sha refers to meat, which can be beef (or more commonly buffalo), pork or chicken, though vegetarian versions of phingsha also exist. Wood ear mushrooms – also known as black cloud fungus, cloud ear and jelly ear due to their shape – are often added too. Personally, I love these mushrooms for their chewy texture and the way sauce clings to their crevasses. In the UK they can be bought dried in Asian grocers or online and need to be rehydrated before cooking.

1. Soak the dried wood ear mushrooms in cold water for 30 minutes. Once fully rehydrated, they will be soft and pliable with a gelatinous texture. Give them a good wash and then halve the mushrooms, or quarter if they are large. If you are using shiitake mushrooms there's no need to soak – simply quarter them.

2. Place the noodles in a heatproof bowl, cover with boiling water and set aside for 6 to 7 minutes. Alternatively, you can boil the noodles for 3 to 5 minutes or according to the packet instructions in a pan, then drain and run under cold water to ensure they don't overcook.

3. Heat the oil in a wide, deep pan and when hot, add the dried and fresh chillies followed by the onion. Keep this moving around the pan for 5 minutes and then add the garlic and ginger to cook for a further 2 minutes.

4. Next add the tomatoes, potatoes and Sichuan peppercorns to the pan. Give everything a good stir and cook for 3 minutes before adding the chicken. Allow the pieces to whiten before adding the white pepper, turmeric, salt and soy sauce. (If you are using shiitake mushrooms, add them now and allow them to soften for 3 to 4 minutes.)

5. Add the rehydrated wood ear mushrooms along with the stock cube and enough water to just cover all the ingredients. Bring to the boil and then simmer gently for 10 minutes, or until the potato is soft.

6. Use scissors to cut the soaked or boiled glass noodles in half, then add them to the pan with the spinach or bok choy if using. Simmer for a final 2 minutes before ladling into bowls.

7. Heat a small pan and add the oil for the topping. When hot, add the sliced shallots and fry gently for 5 minutes. As they begin to bronze, add the spring onions. Mix well, then drizzle a teaspoon on top of each bowlful for added crunch. This also works really well with a drizzle of my Chilli Oil on top (see page 46) for an extra kick.

Notes: Glass noodles – also called bean thread or cellophane noodles – are made with mung bean, sweet potato or potato starch and water. They are semi-translucent when dry and become almost see-through when cooked, hence their name. You can replace them with rice vermicelli noodles, although the texture and flavour of the dish will be a little different.

Oven-Baked Shaphalay

Preparation time: 15 minutes
Cooking time: 35-40 minutes
Makes 14

3 tbsp vegetable, sunflower or rapeseed oil

1 fresh chilli, finely chopped

1 medium onion, finely chopped

3 garlic cloves, finely chopped or 1 heaped tsp garlic paste

1 tsp finely grated fresh ginger or ginger paste

400g minced lamb, beef or chicken, or crumbled paneer or tofu

1 tsp Sichuan peppercorns, crushed

2 tbsp light soy sauce

½ tsp fine salt

¼ tsp caster sugar (optional)

70g finely chopped spinach or cabbage

2 x 320g packs of ready-rolled puff pastry

1 egg, whisked or a dash of milk

These savoury semi-circular pasties look very similar to a Cornish pasty in the UK and a *kachori* in Kolkata, India. Sha means meat and phalay means bread. They are Tibetan in origin and a typical street food in the northeastern parts of India – if you head to Darjeeling, Kalimpong or Sikkim you will find these tasty snacks everywhere. Typically, they are filled with spiced lamb, beef or chicken mince and cabbage but they work equally well with a vegetarian or vegan filling if you prefer to use paneer or tofu. While shaphalay are usually fried, I have opted for the healthier option of oven-baking and using store-bought puff pastry for ease.

1. Heat the oil in a wide pan and then add the chilli and onion. Allow them to soften over the next 4 minutes and then add the garlic and ginger. Stir and cook for another minute.

2. Add the mince, paneer or tofu and cook for 5 minutes before stirring in the Sichuan peppercorns, light soy sauce, salt and sugar (if using).

3. Mix well and then add the spinach or cabbage. Simmer gently for the next 5 minutes. Make sure that any liquid released by the mince, paneer or tofu has been absorbed and the filling is dry. Taste to check the seasoning, adjust as needed, then leave to cool.

4. Unroll the puff pastry and use an upside-down saucer or small side plate as a template to cut out neat rounds of pastry approximately 5 inches in diameter with a sharp knife.

5. Place two tablespoons of the filling just off centre on each round of pastry. Use your finger to lightly wet the top edge and then bring one side of the pastry over the filling to encase it and create a half-moon shape. Press down so that the edges stick together and use a fork to seal the parcel by gently pressing the tines into the pastry.

6. Repeat to make all the shaphalay, then brush the tops with the whisked egg or milk, which helps to give the pastry a bronze glow when baked.

7. Bake the shaphalay in a preheated oven at 180°C/160°C fan/350°F/Gas 4 for 20 minutes. Serve them alongside some Himalayan Hot Sauce (see page 176).

Notes: To make your own chicken mince, simply blitz boneless and skinless chicken thighs in a powerful food processor until the meat has just broken down. If you want to freeze the shaphalay, place them on a baking tray after Step 5 and freeze uncovered until solid, then transfer to resealable bags and store in the freezer until needed. They can be egg-washed and cooked from frozen but may need a little longer in the oven, up to 30 minutes in total. If you prefer, you can also make these pasties with filo pastry instead of puff.

Aloo Dum

Preparation time: 10 minutes
Cooking time: 18 minutes
Serves 4

500g potatoes, peeled and cut into
1-inch cubes

2 tbsp vegetable, sunflower or
rapeseed oil

¼ tsp fenugreek seeds

1 tsp nigella seeds

½ - 1 tsp dried chilli flakes

4 garlic cloves, finely chopped

½ tsp Kashmiri chilli powder

1 tsp ground turmeric

1 tsp fine salt

250ml water

This is an absolute favourite of the Himalayan people. Versions of the dish stretch from the Kashmir Valley to Nepal, with many variations along the way. Traditionally it contains no tomato, onion, garlic or ginger, and yet the Punjabi version includes all of the above. My recipe stays closer to the traditional, more paired back style, although I have added garlic. It is very quick to cook once the potatoes have been boiled.

1. Begin by boiling the potatoes for around 10 minutes or until they are just soft but not falling apart. Drain and then set aside. You can do this advance and then store them in the fridge until you are ready to prepare the dish.

2. Heat the oil in a pan and then add the fenugreek and nigella seeds, dried chilli flakes and garlic. Stir for 10 seconds and then add the ground spices. Stir for a further 10 seconds, then add the boiled potatoes.

3. Coat the potatoes in the oil and spices and then add the salt. Add the water and simmer for 7 minutes, by which time the gravy will have thickened and should cling to the potatoes.

Sikkim Nettle and Spinach Soup

Preparation time: 10 minutes
Cooking time: 15 minutes
Serves 4-6

2 tbsp vegetable, sunflower or rapeseed oil

1 medium onion, finely chopped

1 tsp fine salt, or to taste

4 garlic cloves, roughly chopped

1-inch piece (15g) of fresh ginger, roughly chopped

1-2 fresh green chillies, roughly chopped (optional)

1 tsp Sichuan peppercorns, lightly crushed

1 litre water

100g nettle leaves

100g fresh or frozen spinach leaves

1 tbsp cornflour

3 tbsp cold water

Juice of ½ a lime

Nettles are a staple food source in Sikkim, northeast India, where they grow wild and plentifully even over the cold winter months. Traditionally, this soup is only made with nettle leaves but as they are seasonal and can be tricky to source in an urban setting, I have added spinach. If you can, I suggest collecting three or four young leaves from the tops of nettle plants, using tongs or gloves to avoid being stung. Once the nettles have been boiled as part of the cooking process, they lose their sting. If you can't find nettles, just replace them with spinach. They are both packed full of nutrients and versatile ingredients, from pakoras and fritters to creamy saag. This soup also features an ingredient popular with Sikkim's neighbouring Tibet – *yerma* (otherwise known as Sichuan peppercorns) are often used to give it that tingly, peppery kick.

1. First, gather your nettle leaves carefully using long tongs or gardening gloves. Aim for plants that are not growing alongside public footpaths or at ground level and pick the younger, smaller leaves at the tops of the stems. Wash the nettle leaves thoroughly when you get home.

2. Heat the oil in a large, deep pot and then add the onion and salt. Allow to soften and lightly bronze over the next 5 minutes.

3. Add the garlic, ginger and chillies (if using) to the onions along with the crushed Sichuan peppercorns. Mix well and cook for 2 to 3 minutes before adding the water.

4. Bring the water to a rolling boil and then carefully add the nettle and spinach leaves. Submerge them and simmer gently for 7 to 8 minutes.

5. Mix the cornflour with the cold water to form a smooth paste, then stir this into the soup and let it thicken.

6. Using a handheld blender, blitz the soup to break down all the ingredients until smooth. Strain the soup if required for an even smoother consistency.

7. Add the lime juice and taste to check the seasoning, adding more salt if required. Divide the soup between bowls and serve hot.

Vegetable Momo

Preparation time: 1 hour
Cooking time: 14 minutes
Makes 27

For the wrappers

180g plain flour

60g cornflour

1 tsp fine salt

2 tsp vegetable, sunflower or rapeseed oil

130ml warm water

For the filling

100g white or red cabbage

80g carrots

1 tsp fine salt

2 spring onions

3 garlic cloves, finely grated

1 tbsp finely grated fresh ginger

1 tsp freshly ground black pepper

30g fresh coriander leaves and stalks

Pinch of MSG or caster sugar

1 tbsp light soy sauce

Undoubtedly the most loved street food snack in Darjeeling, the momo (also known as a dumpling) has roots in both Nepal and Tibet. They are also very much part of the Indo-Chinese community in Kolkata – see page 26 for a chicken version. While making your own wrappers may seem daunting, they are pretty straightforward to make. If you are short of time though, store-bought wrappers work well, you just need to dab a little water around the circumference to help seal them. Momos freeze well, so you can make a batch to eat and to keep.

1. To make the wrappers, sift both flours into a bowl, then add the salt and half the oil. Mix well, then gradually add the warm water until the mixture comes together into a dough.

2. Turn out the dough onto a clean surface and knead it for 3 to 5 minutes. Shape into a ball, coat with the remaining teaspoon of oil, then place back in the bowl and cover with a damp cloth while you make the filling.

3. Finely grate the cabbage and carrots. You can use a box grater, or if you have a Magimix the grater disc works really well. Place in a bowl, cover with the salt and leave for 10 to 15 minutes to draw out the water from the cabbage and carrots.

4. Meanwhile, finely slice the spring onions and finely chop the fresh coriander so all your filling ingredients are prepped.

5. Return to the cabbage and carrot and use your hand to squeeze out the moisture. Pour the liquid out of the bowl and repeat a couple of times.

6. Combine all the ingredients for the filling in a blender and pulse a couple of times until everything comes together. Turn out into a bowl and set aside.

7. Take 13g of the dough and roll out to form a disc 4 inches in diameter and no thicker than a penny. You can use an upturned glass or a cookie cutter to cut out the rounds. I make each momo one at a time, keeping the uncut dough covered to stop it drying out.

8. Place 1 heaped teaspoon of the filling into the centre of the wrapper. You now have 4 options for shaping the momo, which are all easy to achieve. (Continued overleaf...)

Vegetable Momo (Continued)

Option 1

Bring the bottom half of the wrapper up towards the top half of the wrapper, enclosing the filling. You can then gently press the opposite sides of the dough together to create a half-moon shape. Once a half-moon has been created, take both corners and bring them round so they meet at the bottom and then slightly cross over, like a tortellini. These dumplings are also known as rosebuds.

Option 2

This method makes a three-pointed momo. Place a teaspoon of filling into the centre of the wrapper and then squeeze the dough together a third of the way up at one end. Then bring the middle of the open part of the wrapper up to the central crease, making a triangle shape with 3 corners. Secure the edges firmly.

Option 3

Start bringing one side of the wrapper up in a pleating motion as if you are bunching the wrapper together. Keep turning, pleating as you go and enclosing the filling until you have run out of dough and created a round momo with a pleated top.

1. Momo can be steamed, fried or boiled, but my preference is to steam them. If you are using a metal steamer, oil the bottom to make it non-stick. If you are using a bamboo steamer, cut out rounds of baking parchment to fit the base.

2. Add water to the steamer and bring to the boil. Place your momos in the steamer, cover with the lid and steam for 14 to 15 minutes. Make sure the water doesn't touch them.

3. To fry the momo, simply add a little oil to a pan with a well-fitting lid and then place the momos in the pan. Allow the bottom of the momos to lightly bronze over a couple of minutes, then add about 50ml of water and cover with the lid to allow it to steam for 4 to 6 minutes, by which time the water will have been absorbed. Try one momo to check the dough is cooked through and steam for a few more minutes if required.

4. To boil the momo, I like to have a vegetable, miso or chicken stock on hand for extra flavour. Add the momo to the hot stock and cook on a medium to low heat for 10 to 15 minutes. You can also cook them from frozen with this method.

5. Serve your momo alongside Himalayan Hot Sauce (see page 176) or homemade chilli oil (see page 46) or simply with soy sauce for dipping into before eating.

Notes: 100g of grated or crumbled paneer or tofu makes a tasty addition to these dumplings. The momo wrappers can be made with 240g of plain flour but I think they taste much better with the cornflour. The wrappers can be frozen, lightly floured so they don't stick together and stored in an airtight freezer bag. You can also freeze the filled momos by placing them on a tray in the freezer for 1 hour and then transferring them to a freezer bag or airtight container for storing.

Himalayan Hot Sauce

Preparation time: 5 minutes
Cooking time: 5 minutes
Makes 1 small bowl

1-3 dried whole red chillies (depending on how hot you like it)

2 medium tomatoes, kept whole

½ small red onion, quartered

2 cloves of garlic, kept whole

½ tsp Sichuan peppercorns

1 tsp fine salt

¼ tsp Kashmiri chilli powder (optional)

1 tbsp sunflower, vegetable or rapeseed oil

Originating from Tibet, this hot sauce is known there as *sepen* and, as many Tibetans reside in northeast India, has crossed borders with them. It is the perfect dipping sauce for momo (dumplings – see pages 26 and 172) and has a delicious tongue-numbing heat from the Sichuan peppercorns – see the supplier directory on page 244 for where to source them.

1. Place the dried chillies in a bowl and cover with boiling water. I always add 3 for a delicious pop of heat, but the quantity is up to you. Leave the chillies to soak for 5 minutes, then drain and discard the water.

2. Heat a small pan of water to boiling point. Use a sharp knife to score a cross in the top and bottom of the tomatoes. Blanch the tomatoes in the boiling water for a minute, then remove the tomatoes and discard the water.

3. Carefully peel the skins off the tomatoes. Discard the skins and chop the tomato flesh into chunks.

4. Using a small blender or wet grinder, blitz all the ingredients except the oil to form a smooth paste.

5. Heat the oil in a small pan and then add the paste. Use a spatula to move the sauce around the pan for a couple of minutes – the heat will remove any raw smell or taste from the onion and garlic.

6. Pour the sauce into a chutney bowl and allow to cool before eating. Perfect with either variety of momo (see pages 26 and 172) and the Shaphalay on page 166.

Notes: If you can't find or don't want to use Sichuan peppercorns, you can use the same quantity of ordinary black peppercorns instead.

Parsi

The Parsi people of Pars (a Sasanian province, now known as Fars) originally came to India in the eighth century, fleeing persecution from their Arab Muslim rulers in modern-day Iran as they were unwilling to convert to Islam. The Parsis are followers of a religion known as Zoroastrianism which dates back to the sixth century BCE, predating both Christianity and Islam, and was the dominant religion in Persia until the advent of Islam in the seventh century.

The Parsis arrived and settled mainly in the states of Gujarat and Maharashtra in western India, where they were granted asylum and accepted by the local priests on the proviso that they came in peace, adopted the local ways when it came to dress, customs and language (Gujarati) and only carried out their own ceremonies involving processions at night. A mantra Zoroastrians hold dear is 'good thoughts, good words, good deeds' and this positive outlook clearly helped them survive and thrive. They assimilated well in their newly adopted land, working hard to establish themselves in a wide range of industries from shipbuilding to agriculture. Following the arrival of the British East India Company in Gujarat in 1608, the Parsis were receptive to European influence, perhaps more so than their Hindu and Muslim counterparts, and this elevated their social profile in some ways. They acted as brokers and mediators to the European traders as they were not restricted by rules associated with caste or diet. When Bom Bahia, part of Bombay's seven islands and what is now Mumbai, was given to the English monarchy by the Portuguese as part of Catherine of Braganza's dowry on her marriage to King Charles II, the Parsis were integral in helping the growing metropolis thrive through their aptitude for commerce.

When looking at Parsi cuisine, I rather like the analogy that Niloufer Ichaporia King makes in her book *My Bombay Kitchen*. She describes it as a 'magpie cuisine' – in other words, taking elements from the Parsis' Persian homeland as well as their adopted home, with its plethora of spices and European influenced dishes. This kaleidoscope of influences have come together to create a modern Parsi cuisine that is constantly evolving. There are common threads running through it though, such as the generous use of eggs, onions, garlic, dried fruit, nuts, chicken and cream. Vegetables were typically used in meat dishes rather than as key ingredients in their own right, though this has changed in recent decades with Parsi vegetarian dishes becoming familiar additions to the dinner table.

Runner Beans with Lamb

Preparation time: 15 minutes
Cooking time: 1 hour (or 35-40
minutes in pressure cooker, see notes
on page 9)
Serves 4

2-3 tbsp vegetable, sunflower or
rapeseed oil

1 tsp ajwain/carom seeds

1 tsp cumin seeds

3 cloves

5 black peppercorns

1 Indian bay leaf (optional)

5 green cardamom pods

2-inch piece of cinnamon or cassia bark

2 large onions, finely chopped

1 tsp fine salt

1 heaped tsp finely grated garlic

1 heaped tsp finely grated fresh ginger

2 large tomatoes, roughly chopped or
puréed

1 tsp Kashmiri chilli powder

1 tsp ground coriander

½ tsp ground turmeric

½ tsp ground cumin

800g lamb neck or shoulder, cut into
2-inch pieces

400ml water

300g runner beans, cut diagonally into
2-inch pieces

3 medium potatoes, halved (optional)

1 tsp garam masala

This tasty Parsi dish is known as *papri ma gosht*, which has a wonderful thyme-like aroma from the ajwain/carom seeds, so it's important not to leave them out! When the Parsis fled Persia (modern-day Iran) they settled in Gujarat, where they were introduced to a vegetable known as *papri*, which looks and tastes similar to a small European runner bean, and began using it in their cooking, often combining it with goat and lamb meat. In India, this recipe is typically made in a pressure cooker to soften the meat to perfection. As pressure cookers are less commonly used in western kitchens, the method I've used here starts on the stove top and then cooks slowly in the oven – or you could use a slow cooker if you wish. If you are able to source *papri* when they are in season, do use them instead of runner beans.

1. Heat the oil in a cast-iron pan and then add the ajwain and cumin seeds, cloves, black peppercorns, Indian bay leaf, green cardamom and cinnamon or cassia. Move everything around the pan for 20 seconds before adding the chopped onion and salt.

2. Allow the onion to lightly bronze over the next 6 to 8 minutes and then add the garlic and ginger. Stir well and cook for another couple of minutes.

3. Next, add the chopped or puréed tomato and simmer for a minute before adding the Kashmiri chilli powder, coriander, turmeric and cumin. Mix well.

4. Add the lamb to the pan and stir well. Simmer gently for 3 to 4 minutes before adding the water. Cover with a lid and transfer to a preheated oven at 180°C/160°C fan/350°F/Gas 4 and cook for 45 minutes.

5. Now add the runner beans and potatoes (if using) to the pan, give everything a good stir and cover with a lid to cook for a further 20 minutes.

6. Finally, add the garam masala and mix well before serving.

Vegetable Dhansak

Preparation time: 15 minutes, plus soaking

Cooking time: 1 hour

Serves 4-6

For the dal

100g red split lentils/masoor dal

100g yellow moong/mung dal

100g yellow toor/pigeon dal or chana dal

½ tsp ground turmeric

1.4 litres water

For the roast veg

Choose 2 or 3 of the following:

1 whole aubergine, 2 large carrots, 250g butternut squash or pumpkin or swede

2 tbsp sunflower, vegetable or rapeseed oil

For the curry base

3-4 tbsp sunflower, vegetable or rapeseed oil

1 large onion, finely chopped

1½ tsp fine salt

3 garlic cloves, finely chopped or grated or 1 heaped tsp garlic paste

2-inch (30g) piece of fresh ginger, finely grated or 1 tsp ginger paste

2 tsp dhansak masala, store-bought or homemade (see page 184)

1 tsp Kashmiri chilli powder

1 tsp ground coriander

½ tsp ground cumin

3 large tomatoes, finely chopped or puréed

200ml water

If there is one recipe that screams Parsi food the loudest, it would undoubtedly be dhansak. Usually made with lamb or chicken, it can be equally delicious with vegetables which is the version I've made here. Dhansak is held in the same esteem as our Sunday roasts are in the UK. Many people are put off making it at home by the amount of ingredients and steps, so I have broken it down and made it easier and quicker, without compromising the flavour.

1. Begin by soaking the three dals in a bowl of water for a couple of hours. After soaking, drain the dal and wash a couple of times in fresh water, pouring the water away gently from the bowl (it's not necessary to use a sieve here).

2. Place the soaked dal in a large deep pan, add the ground turmeric and cover with the 1.4 litres of water. Cook on a medium heat for 30 to 45 minutes or until the dal is completely soft. While it cooks, skim off and discard any scum that rises to the surface.

3. To check the lentils are done, take a little of the toor or chana dal (this takes the longest to cook) and pinch it between your thumb and forefinger. It should be completely soft. Add a little more water if the dal begins to stick to the bottom of the pan. If you have a pressure cooker, it will take no longer than 20 minutes to cook.

4. Dice your chosen vegetables into bite-size cubes, spread them out on a baking tray and drizzle with the oil. Roast the veg in a preheated oven at 200°C/180°C fan/400°F/Gas 6 for 25 to 30 minutes, until soft. Remove from the oven and set aside.

5. To make the curry base, first heat the oil in a medium pan. Add the onion and half a teaspoon of the salt, cook on a medium to low heat for 10 minutes until bronzed and then add the garlic and ginger to cook for another 2 minutes.

6. Add a little more oil to the pan before stirring in the dhansak masala, Kashmiri chilli powder, ground coriander and cumin followed by the tomatoes and simmer gently for 3 to 4 minutes. Add a little water if it is catching at the bottom or looking dry.

7. Now pour the contents of the frying pan into the dal, then rinse the pan with the water and pour this in too so none of the flavour is lost.

8. Add the roasted vegetables to the dal mixture and use a potato masher or handheld blender to break them down, leaving some pieces intact to add texture.

9. Taste to check the seasoning, add a little more salt as required and give the dhansak a good stir.

10. Serve alongside the Parsi 'Brown' Rice on page 186 and Allegra's Kachumber Salad (see page 76).

Notes: If you can't find all three dals listed in the ingredients, you can just use equal amounts of two dals to make up the total quantity.

Dhansak Masala

Preparation time: 10 minutes
Cooking time: 12 minutes
Makes 1 jam jar

10g dried lime peel

10g dried orange peel

4 tbsp coriander seeds

2 tbsp cumin seeds

1 tbsp black peppercorns

1 tsp fenugreek seeds

1 tsp caraway seeds

1 tsp cloves

1 tsp white poppy seeds

1 tsp black mustard seeds

6 green cardamom pods

20 fresh or frozen curry leaves

2 x 2-inch pieces of cinnamon or cassia bark

1 tsp ground turmeric

While researching for this chapter, I came across a few dhansak masala recipes, but many circled back to the one Bichoo J. Manekshaw talks about in her book *Parsi Food and Customs*. She grew up praising the one her maternal grandmother made until she met a Mrs Aloo Shroff, whose masala was far superior. I have adapted the recipe as the original would produce such a large amount, I cannot imagine anyone cooking dhansak enough times in one year to finish it off. I've also omitted Indian bay leaves (known as *tej patta*) as I know these can be tricky to find. I think the two ingredients that set Manekshaw's recipe apart are dried orange and lime peel.

1. If you want to make the dried peel at home rather than using store-bought, begin by using a potato peeler to peel strips of zest from a lime and an orange.

2. Place the peel into a preheated oven at 180°C/160°C fan/350°F/Gas 4 for 10 minutes, after which time it will have begun to shrivel and dry out.

3. Heat a large frying pan and then add the coriander and cumin seeds, peppercorns, fenugreek and caraway seeds and cloves. Move it all around the pan for a minute before adding the poppy and mustard seeds, green cardamom, curry leaves and cinnamon or cassia. Stir for another minute. This will awaken all the spices prior to blending them.

4. Pour the contents of the pan into a spice grinder – do this in two batches if your spice grinder is too small.

5. Add both dried peels and the ground turmeric, then blitz to form a fine powder. Store the masala in a sterilised glass jar, out of direct sunlight, and ideally use within 6 months.

Parsi 'Brown' Rice

Preparation time: 30 minutes
Cooking time: 25-30 minutes
Serves 4

200g white basmati rice

2 tbsp vegetable, sunflower or rapeseed oil, or ghee (or 1 tbsp of each)

1 large onion, finely sliced

1 tsp sugar

2-inch piece of cinnamon or cassia bark

4 green cardamom pods

3 black peppercorns

4 cloves

400ml water

1 tsp fine salt

Despite the name, this dish is made with white basmati rice and not brown – it's the caramelised onion that gives it that moniker, along with adding delicate sweet notes. I go lightly on the sugar, although when I was researching this recipe many versions I found used 2 tablespoons or more, which I think is excessive. This rice is traditionally served alongside dhansak and a kachumber salad but it goes equally well with many of the meat and fish dishes in this book. It's easy to master and something that I hope you'll return to time and time again.

1. First, wash the rice with 2 or 3 changes of water, then place in a bowl, cover with fresh water and leave to soak for 30 minutes. After this time, drain thoroughly and set aside.

2. Heat the oil and/or ghee in a pan, then add the onion and cook on a medium to low heat for around 10 minutes. As it starts to lightly bronze, add the sugar and stir well. Allow it to caramelise, which will take a few minutes.

3. Remove a spoonful of the onions and set aside to garnish the finished dish. Now add all the whole spices to the remaining onions in the pan and mix well. After 30 seconds, add the prepared rice and gently fold in to combine everything.

4. Pour in the water and scatter in the salt. Allow the water to come to the boil and then turn the heat down, cover and leave to cook for 10 minutes.

5. After this time, turn off the heat and allow to steam for a further 5 minutes without removing the lid.

6. To serve, gently fluff up the rice with a fork and decant to a platter or bowl, then scatter with the reserved caramelised onions.

Jardaloo Salli Boti

Preparation time: 15 minutes
Cooking time: 1 hour 30 minutes
Serves 4-6

This well-known lamb curry literally translates as apricots (jardaloo), potato straws (salli), lamb (boti) and is always prepared as part of a Parsi wedding feast. It's a delight for the senses and a nod to the Parsi ancestry in Persia with the delicate sweetness of apricots, which are puréed.

3 tbsp vegetable, sunflower or rapeseed oil, plus extra for deep frying if making your own potato straws

2-inch piece of cinnamon or cassia bark

5 green cardamom pods

4 cloves

2-3 dried whole red chillies

2 large white onions, finely sliced

1 tsp fine salt

2 tsp finely grated fresh ginger or ginger paste

2 tsp finely grated garlic or garlic paste

4 large tomatoes (300g), finely chopped or blended

½ - 1 tsp Kashmiri chilli powder

½ tsp ground turmeric

1 tsp ground coriander

1 tsp ground cumin

1 tsp garam masala

1kg lamb neck or shoulder, diced into bite-size pieces

10 dried whole apricots, puréed with a little water

1 tbsp white wine or apple cider vinegar

300ml water

1 large potato, peeled and cut into thin straws (or store-bought potato straw crisps)

½ tsp fine salt

Fresh coriander, to serve

1. Heat the oil in a deep pan and then add the cinnamon or cassia, green cardamom, cloves and dried chillies. Stir for 30 seconds before adding the onion and salt.

2. Cook on a medium to low heat to allow the onions to bronze. This will take 10 to 15 minutes so stir intermittently to make sure they don't catch.

3. Once the onion has bronzed, add the ginger and garlic. After a couple of minutes, add the tomatoes and allow them to soften, adding a splash of water if it catches on the bottom or looks too dry.

4. After 4 to 5 minutes, add the ground spices and then the lamb. Turn the heat up and seal the lamb so that it lightly browns over the next 10 minutes.

5. Stir in the apricot purée, vinegar and water and then cover the pan with a lid. You can either cook this on the hob over a medium heat for 50 minutes to 1 hour until the meat has softened, or transfer to a preheated oven at 200°C/180°C fan/400°F/Gas 6 to cook for the same amount of time.

6. If making your own potato straws, soak the potato in cold water for 5 minutes, stirring gently to wash off the excess starch. Drain and then pat dry with kitchen paper.

7. To deep fry the potato straws, half-fill a small pan with oil and heat for 5 minutes. Carefully place one potato straw into the oil and if it immediately begins to fizzle, the temperature is high enough. Fry the potato straws in batches for a couple of minutes until they bronze and crisp up, then remove with a slotted spoon and place on dry kitchen paper to soak up any excess oil. Sprinkle with a little salt while hot.

8. To serve, divide the lamb curry between bowls and scatter with a sprinkling of potato straws and some fresh coriander.

Steamed Fish in Coriander, Mint and Coconut Chutney

Preparation time: 20 minutes
Cooking time: 15 minutes
Serves 4-6

4-6 white firm fish fillets

½ tsp Kashmiri chilli powder

½ tsp ground turmeric

½ tsp fine salt

Juice of ½ a lemon or lime

For the chutney

100g finely grated fresh or frozen coconut, or desiccated coconut

65g fresh coriander, leaves and stalks

25g fresh mint leaves, leaves only

3 fresh green chillies (use fewer and/or deseed for less heat)

2-inch (30g) piece of fresh ginger

5 garlic cloves, peeled

Juice of 1 lemon or lime

1 tbsp caster sugar

½ tsp fine salt, or to taste

Ice-cold water, as required

To cook

4-6 large pieces of baking paper, banana leaf or fig leaves, to wrap the fish

Kitchen string, to tie the parcels if needed

Steaming fish in a fresh, zingy, sweet, salty chutney is a favourite among the Parsi community. Traditionally it is called *patra ni maachi* which simply translates to 'fish wrapped in a leaf' – typically this is a banana leaf but because these aren't always easily sourced in the UK, baking parchment is my go-to, or fig leaves in the summer. In India, pomfret is typically used to make this dish, but any firm fish such as sea bass, sea bream, cod or tilapia would work equally well.

1. Place the fish in a bowl, add the Kashmiri chilli powder, ground turmeric, salt and lemon or lime juice and mix well. Cover and set aside while you prepare the chutney.

2. Place all the chutney ingredients in a blender and blitz until smooth. Add a little ice-cold water to loosen the mixture slightly and retain the bright green colour. The chutney needs to be quite thick so that it can be spread over the fish without running off.

3. If you are using baking paper, simply cut into large squares big enough to wrap the fish. If you are using banana leaf rather than baking paper, remove the spines of the leaf and cut into equal pieces big enough to wrap your fish in, then place over a heat source (such as the flame on a gas hob) for a few seconds so it softens and becomes easier to fold. If you are using fig leaves, give them a good wash and then dry thoroughly.

4. Place a good dollop of the chutney in the centre of each square and place the fish on top. Spoon over more chutney so that the fish is completely covered.

5. Wrap the fish as you would a parcel, so that no fish is exposed. You may find you don't need to use string to secure the parcel if you have folded the ends tightly but if you think it might unravel, use string to hold the paper or leaf in place.

6. If steaming the fish, place the parcels in a steamer with the lid on and cook for 15 minutes. If baking, place the parcels on a baking tray and cook for 15 minutes in a preheated oven at 180°C/160°C fan/350°F/Gas 4.

7. Place the unopened parcels on individual plates for diners to unwrap themselves and enjoy with some rice on the side and a wedge of lemon or lime for squeezing over.

Sweet and Sour Prawn Patio

**Preparation time: 10 minutes (longer
if you prepare the prawns yourself)
Cooking time: 20 minutes
Serves 4**

600g large raw prawns, cleaned, peeled
and deveined

½ tsp Kashmiri chilli powder

½ tsp ground turmeric

Juice of ½ a lemon

¼ tsp fine salt

3 tbsp sunflower, vegetable or
rapeseed oil

1 large onion, finely chopped

½ tsp fine salt, or to taste

10-15 fresh or frozen curry leaves
(optional)

2 dried whole red chillies, broken in
half

1 heaped tsp finely grated garlic or 2
garlic cloves, finely chopped

1 tsp ground coriander

3 large fresh tomatoes, puréed

1 tomato, finely chopped

1 tsp jaggery or fine sugar

1 tbsp cider vinegar or balsamic vinegar

Small handful of fresh coriander,
chopped

Prawn patio is a much-loved Parsi dish that combines sweet, sour and spicy elements. It reminds me of the Bengali prawn curry – minus the coconut – in my first cookbook and is quick and easy to make, perfect for a midweek meal. The sour flavours come from the vinegar and lemon juice – in Gujarat, a very particular cane sugar vinegar is added, but as this is hard to source elsewhere, I suggest using cider vinegar or even a dash of balsamic vinegar.

1. In a bowl, mix the prepared prawns with the Kashmiri chilli powder, ground turmeric, lemon juice and salt. Make sure they are coated thoroughly and then set aside.

2. Heat the oil in a pan, then add the onion, salt, curry leaves (if using) and dried chillies. Allow this to lightly bronze over the next 6 minutes.

3. Stir in the garlic and cook for a couple of minutes before adding the ground coriander.

4. Add the puréed tomatoes, stir well and then cover for a couple of minutes before adding the chopped tomato, jaggery or sugar and vinegar.

5. Add the marinated prawns and stir well to cover them in the spiced tomato base. Sprinkle in the fresh coriander, cover with the lid and cook for another 6 to 7 minutes.

6. Serve the prawn patio alongside the Parsi 'Brown' Rice on page 186.

Mori Dar

Preparation time: 10 minutes, plus soaking

Cooking time: 1 hour 10 minutes

Serves 6

300g yellow toor dal/dar

1.5 litres cold water

1 tsp fine salt, or to taste

1 tbsp ghee or neutral oil

1 tsp cumin seeds

5 garlic cloves, thinly sliced

3 green chillies, slit lengthways (optional)

1 tsp ground turmeric

Parsis call dal *dar*, which is a lentil soup that can be made thicker or thinner in consistency according to your preference. This version is typically mashed or blitzed for a smoother texture and is a simple dal that is very easy to prepare and eaten on auspicious days. Toor dal, also called pigeon peas, are the most popular lentils in Parsi cuisine, but if you can't find them you can also make this with chana, masoor (red split lentils) or yellow moong/mung.

1. Place the yellow toor dal in a bowl, cover with cold water and leave to soak for a few hours or overnight.

2. Drain the soaked lentils, place them in a deep pan and cover with the 1.5 litres of fresh water. Bring to the boil. Simmer for 45 minutes to 1 hour, or until the dal is soft when pinched between your thumb and forefinger.

3. Use a potato masher or stick blender to make it smoother in consistency. The texture of this dal is typically similar to a purée, but you can leave it chunkier if you prefer.

4. Add the salt and taste to check the seasoning and adjust accordingly. I always season lentils once cooked, so that I can check the taste and get the right balance.

5. In a separate pan, heat the ghee or oil and then add the cumin seeds, sliced garlic and green chillies, if using. This is called tempering and the Parsis refer to it as *vaghar*. Keep the heat low so that the garlic lightly bronzes but does not burn.

6. Pour half the contents of the tempering pan into the dal, then add the ground turmeric and give it a good stir. You may find you need to add a little more water to loosen the dal.

7. Simmer gently for a few minutes and then pour the remaining tempering ingredients over the top of the dal when serving.

Eggs on Okra

Preparation time: 15 minutes
Cooking time: 15 minutes
Serves 2-4

2 tbsp vegetable, rapeseed or
sunflower oil

1 tsp cumin seeds

1 medium onion, finely chopped

½ tsp fine salt

2 garlic cloves, roughly chopped

300g fresh or frozen okra, thinly sliced
into rounds

1 tsp ground coriander

½ tsp ground turmeric

½ tsp ground cumin

4 eggs

½ tsp freshly ground black pepper

Fresh coriander, to serve (optional)

The Parsi are big egg eaters. Eggs are so auspicious and revered that apparently they are waved around the heads of special guests as they enter the threshold and are broken on door frames to ward off evil. This dish is commonly known as *bheeda par eeda* and is the Parsi equivalent to a shakshuka, of sorts. I know that okra divides people due to its texture but I urge you to give this a go. Typically, it is eaten for breakfast but would also be a great brunch dish. Okra is now available in some of the large supermarkets so do keep an eye out for it.

1. Heat the oil in a large skillet or frying pan. Add the cumin seeds, then add the onion and salt. Move this around the pan for 4 to 5 minutes before adding the garlic.

2. Cook for a couple of minutes before adding the sliced okra. Mix well, then add the ground spices and use a spatula to stir them in thoroughly.

3. Cover the pan with a lid and cook for 6 to 7 minutes, stirring intermittently. After this time, the okra will have lightly bronzed. Break the eggs on top of the okra, sprinkle with the freshly ground black pepper and cover again with the lid.

4. Let the eggs steam under the lid – they should be cooked within 3 minutes. Serve immediately with a scattering of fresh coriander on top if you like.

Mulligatawny Parsi Style

Preparation time: 15 minutes
Cooking time: 40 minutes
Serves 6

2 tbsp vegetable, sunflower or
rapeseed oil

1 white onion, finely chopped

1 tsp fine salt

450g chicken thighs, skinned and diced
into small bite-size cubes

1.3 litres water, or chicken or vegetable
stock

150ml coconut milk

200g cooked basmati rice

Lime wedges, to serve

For the dry masala

2-inch piece of cinnamon or cassia bark

6 black peppercorns

4 cloves

1 tbsp coriander seeds

1 tbsp white poppy seeds

1 tbsp uncooked basmati rice

1 tbsp slivered almonds

1 heaped tsp cumin seeds

½ tsp ground turmeric

For the wet masala

Handful of fresh coriander leaves and
stems, roughly chopped (approx. 20g)

2-3 fresh green chillies, or to taste

1-inch (15g) piece of fresh ginger

4 garlic cloves

The observant among you may have noticed that this book already includes a recipe for Mulligatawny, on page 64 in the Anglo-Indian chapter. I've included both versions deliberately so you can experiment with making both and seeing which style you prefer. This slightly spicier recipe is inspired by the one from Niloufer Ichaporia King's book *My Bombay Kitchen: Traditional and Modern Parsi Home Cooking*. It's a complete meal in a bowl, or you could serve smaller portions as a starter for a larger feast.

1. Begin by making the dry masala. Warm a dry frying pan and toast everything except the turmeric for 1 minute, keeping it all moving. Pour into a spice grinder and allow to cool for a few minutes before adding the turmeric. Pulse to form a ground masala.

2. For the wet masala, put all the ingredients in a wet grinder with a splash of water and blitz to form a smooth paste. Add the ground masala to the wet grinder and blitz again to allow all the ingredients to come together, forming a green masala paste.

3. In a deep pan, heat the oil and add the onion and salt. Allow this to lightly bronze over the next 6 to 8 minutes.

4. Add the masala paste to the pan and stir well before adding the chicken, coating it in the masala. Add the water or stock and simmer gently for 20 minutes.

5. Finally, add the coconut milk and simmer for a further 10 minutes, keeping the heat low.

6. To serve, place a couple of tablespoons of the cooked rice in each bowl, followed by a few ladles of the soup and a lime wedge on the side.

Sweet and Sour Vegetable Stew

Preparation time: 20 minutes
Cooking time: 40 minutes
Serves 4-6

For the roast veg

250g carrots

250g sweet potatoes

250g turnip or swede

250g cauliflower, chopped into small florets

2 tbsp olive oil

2 tsp Parsi sambar masala (see page 202)

For the curry base

3 tbsp sunflower, vegetable or rapeseed oil

2 medium onions, finely sliced

1 tsp salt, or to taste

1 heaped tsp finely grated garlic

1 heaped tsp finely grated fresh ginger

5 large tomatoes, finely chopped or puréed

1 tsp ground turmeric

1 tsp Kashmiri chilli powder

1 tbsp Parsi sambar masala (see page 202)

1 tbsp white wine or apple cider vinegar

1 tsp caster sugar

200g green beans, chopped into 1-inch pieces

200g frozen peas

300ml water

Handful of fresh coriander leaves and stalks, roughly chopped

1 sprig of fresh mint, roughly chopped

Traditionally, Parsi cuisine always paired vegetables with meat or fish but more recently, vegetarian dishes have begun to shine in their own right. This one is often included as part of a wedding banquet and indeed is often referred to as *lagan nu stew* meaning 'wedding stew'. Typically, each vegetable is shallow fried individually, however, for ease and a healthier take, I have opted to roast the sweet potatoes, carrots, turnip and cauliflower before adding them to the spiced tomato curry base.

1. Preheat the oven to 200°C/180°C fan/400°F/Gas 6 while you peel and chop the carrots, sweet potatoes and turnip or swede into 1-inch cubes. Place these on a baking tray along with the cauliflower florets, then coat all the vegetables with the olive oil and Parsi sambar masala. Rub in well, then roast in the oven for 30 minutes.

2. Meanwhile, heat the oil in a large wide pan and then add the onion and salt to cook for 6 to 8 minutes until lightly bronzed.

3. Add the garlic and ginger, then stir for 2 minutes before adding the tomatoes. Allow this mixture to soften over the next 3 to 4 minutes, then add the turmeric, Kashmiri chilli powder and Parsi sambar masala. Mix well to distribute the spices evenly.

4. Now add the vinegar, sugar, green beans and peas, followed by the water. Simmer for 5 minutes.

5. Add the roasted vegetables to the pan and mix into the spiced tomato base. Cover with a lid and simmer gently for 10 minutes, adding a splash more water as required.

6. Finally, fold in the fresh coriander and mint. Taste to check the seasoning and add a little more salt or sugar if required before serving.

Parsi Sambar Masala

Preparation time: 5 minutes
Makes I small pot

7 dried whole red chillies (use Kashmiri chillies for less heat)

5 black peppercorns

4 cloves

2 star anise

2-inch piece of cinnamon or cassia bark

2 tsp black mustard seeds

I tsp white sesame seeds

½ tbsp fenugreek seeds

½ tsp fine salt

½ tsp asafoetida powder

I tbsp vegetable, sunflower or rapeseed oil

When researching this chapter, I came across several books that spoke about Parsi sambar masala but didn't elaborate on the exact ingredients it contained. When I did come across a recipe, I realised that they all led back to the one that Bhicoo J. Manekshaw talks about in her book *Parsi Food and Customs*. I have adapted her recipe to make a smaller quantity and perhaps an easier approach for making this at home. It's quite different from the sambar masala in my first book, which was more of a South Indian sambar containing lentils as well as spices.

1. In a spice grinder, combine all the ingredients except the salt, asafoetida and oil and grind them into a fine masala.

2. Place the ground masala into a bowl, add the salt and mix thoroughly. Make a well in the centre of the masala and add the asafoetida to this without mixing.

3. Heat the oil and then pour it over the asafoetida. Stir to combine everything until the masala has a slightly crumbly appearance.

4. Allow the masala to cool and then transfer to a glass jar for sealing and storing.

Notes: I couldn't find an explanation for the oil being added in this way during my research, but my guess is that the flavour profile of asafoetida (also known as 'devil's dung stinking gum') changes when the oil hits it, becoming garlicky and more palatable.

Wedding Pickle

Preparation time: 15 minutes
Cooking time: 15 minutes
Makes 1 jar

350g carrots, peeled and finely grated

1 tsp fine salt

15g fresh ginger, peeled and cut into thin batons

2 garlic cloves, peeled and cut into thin batons

1 tsp cumin seeds

4 cloves

6 black peppercorns

2-inch piece of cinnamon or cassia bark

5 green cardamom pods, husks removed

1 tsp Kashmiri chilli powder

½ tsp garam masala

100g jaggery or brown sugar

100ml apple cider, white wine or red wine vinegar

100g mixed dried fruit (see notes)

½ tsp fine salt, or to taste

This Parsi pickle, known as *lagan nu achar*, is an absolute staple in the home and at every Parsi wedding. It combines grated carrots with dried fruits – such as raisins, dates, figs and apricots – and a medley of spices, jaggery (or light brown sugar) and of course vinegar. It balances sweetness, sourness and spice which encapsulates and complements Parsi food perfectly.

1. Place the grated carrot in a mixing bowl and add the fine salt. Mix well and then set aside for 30 minutes. After this time, use your hands to squeeze out all the water that will have been released from the carrots and discard the liquid.

2. Without turning on the heat, place the carrots in a large pan with the ginger and garlic.

3. In a pestle and mortar, grind the cumin seeds, cloves, black peppercorns, cinnamon or cassia and green cardamom seeds to a powder, then add this to the carrots in the pan.

4. Add the Kashmiri chilli powder and garam masala to the pan, then mix everything together until thoroughly combined.

5. Now turn on the heat and add the jaggery or sugar, followed by the vinegar. Mix well. From the point you turn the heat on, the pickle takes no more than 15 minutes to cook.

6. Stir the pickle as it cooks. After 10 minutes, add the dried fruit and salt. If it seems to catch on the bottom of the pan, add a small splash of water to loosen slightly.

7. After 15 minutes on the heat, taste the pickle to check the seasoning and add more salt if required. All the liquid and juices should have been absorbed.

8. Transfer the pickle to a sterilised glass jar, seal with the lid and leave to cool. Store out of direct sunlight in a cool place. It will last for 1 to 2 months if the jar is airtight.

Notes: I recommend choosing three of the following dried fruits to use in this recipe: apricots, dates, figs, prunes, raisins, sultanas. Chop anything larger than a sultana into similar size pieces.

Ricotta and Cardamom Teacake

Preparation time: 15 minutes
Cooking time: 40 minutes
Makes 1 cake

120g granulated sugar

160g unsalted butter, at room temperature

200g ricotta, strained or mawa (see above)

3 eggs

160g plain flour

1 tsp baking powder

1 tsp ground cardamom

½ tsp vanilla extract

70ml semi-skimmed or full-fat milk

1 tbsp roughly chopped pistachios, plus extra slivered pistachios for serving

20g slivered almonds

In the old Irani cafés in Mumbai, there is one particular cake that oozes with nostalgia: mawa cake. Mawa, also known as *khoya*, are milk solids found in several Indian desserts, such as *barfi* and *besan ladoo*. They can be made at home, although it does take time to evaporate full-fat milk until only the milk solids remain, requiring a lot of stirring and patience. You can purchase mawa at some Asian grocers or use milk powder but personally, I prefer to use ricotta, which is easy to come by and equally delicious.

1. Preheat your oven to 180°C/160°C fan/350°F/Gas 4.
2. In a large mixing bowl, cream the sugar and butter with a handheld mixer or a spatula.
3. Add the ricotta or mawa and lightly whisk on a low speed, if using a mixer. Add one egg at a time and keep mixing until combined before adding the next.
4. In a separate bowl, combine the flour, baking powder and cardamon.
5. Add the dry ingredients to the wet ingredients in stages, gently folding in each batch.
6. Add the vanilla extract and milk to the batter, folding the liquids in with a spatula to keep the mixture light and airy. Finally, fold in the chopped pistachios.
7. Grease and line a 7.5-inch springform cake tin or an 8–9-inch loaf tin with baking parchment and pour in the cake mixture. Smooth out the surface.
8. Place the tin in the centre of the oven and bake for 40 minutes if using a round tin or longer in a loaf tin, up to an hour in total. Check the cake at 10-minute intervals after the initial baking time by inserting a skewer in the centre – if it comes out clean, the cake is done. Scatter the slivered almonds evenly on top about 20 minutes before the cake is done so they become nicely toasted.
9. Remove from the oven and leave the cake in the tin for 10 minutes before using a sharp knife to loosen the edges, then turn it out onto a wire rack to cool.
10. This is delicious eaten warm or at room temperature, with a dollop of yoghurt or cream alongside and some extra slivered pistachio sprinkled on top.

Notes: Because of the ricotta, this cake has a denser, closer texture than ordinary sponge. For a lighter cake, you can replace half the butter with vegetable oil. For an egg-free version, use 100g of plain yoghurt in place of the eggs.

Mughal

The Mughal empire was vast, stretching across the Indian subcontinent from present-day Pakistan to Bangladesh, as far south as Hyderabad in India and as far north as Afghanistan. The empire encompassed many ethnic groups, languages and religions including Afghan, Turkish, Kashmiri, Persian and Punjabi. These created a heady cocktail of culinary techniques and flavours within Mughal cuisine.

Established in 1526, the Mughal empire originated with the Timurid prince Babur, who defeated Ibrahim Lodi at the Battle of Panipat. Babur hailed from Andijan, the oldest city in modern-day Uzbekistan, and was descended on his father's side from Timur, also known as Tamerlane, who built an empire in the fourteenth century around what is now Afghanistan, Iran and central Asia. His maternal ancestry included Genghis Khan, the all-powerful Mongol warrior, and in honour of his mother's lineage, Babur used the Persian name for Mongol – Mughal – to name his own fledgling empire. Over the course of the next 300 years, 17 Mughal emperors ruled until the British East India Company took control in the mid-nineteenth century, exiling the last of them, Bahadur Shah Zafar II, to Rangoon in Burma, modern-day Myanmar.

These new rulers brought many new influences to the region in terms of art, culture, language and, of course, cuisine. The food was fragrantly spiced, with heady notes of cardamom, rose petals, cloves and cinnamon, and yet it was not spicy. Chilli powder, turmeric and garlic were rarely used to begin with, although by the sixteenth century they began to make appearances in some dishes. The use of dried fruit and nuts in both savoury and sweet dishes was commonplace and marinating meats in yoghurt and spices was a popular technique. While the Mughal emperors were Muslim, the chefs in the royal courts were both Muslim and Hindu, so influences from both religions can be found in the preparation of Mughlai cuisine. Beef and pork were omitted on the religious grounds of the majority but lamb, chicken, game and fish (fresh and saltwater) were much enjoyed. Vegetables and lentils also featured often, in part due to the influence of several Mughal rulers who were fully or partially vegetarian for much of their lives. Aurangzeb, the sixth ruler, much preferred lighter vegetarian meals compared to his predecessors. Saffron also arrived with the Mughals, adding its distinctive flavour and vibrant colour to their dishes.

The wives of the emperors also played their part in influencing the cuisine of the royal courts. Many of these women were Hindu princesses from Rajput families, creating alliances and harmony with the powerful Rajput for the Mughal emperors while incidentally adding Hindu touches in the kitchen. The five-lentil dish known as *panchemel dal*, for example, was introduced to the royal court by Emperor Akbar's wife, Johda, during the late sixteenth century.

It was during the peaceful reign of Shah Jahan – creator of India's architectural jewel, the Taj Mahal, and the Red Fort Complex in Delhi – that the food of the royal court made its way to the local people and into the markets. He moved his capital from Agra to Delhi and renamed it Shahjahanabad. Arts flourished under his reign and there was much pomp and grandeur when it came to food preparation and consumption. The cuisine of the Mughals was very laborious in terms of time and ingredients, but as this style of cooking filtered down to the wider population the recipes were altered and short cuts adopted to suit home kitchens and feed families rather than entire courts.

We can get a glimpse into the imperial kitchens of the Mughal courts thanks to a detailed manuscript written during Emperor Jahangir's time called *Nuskha-e-Shahjahani*, a copy of which can be found in the British Library. This seventeenth-century manuscript has been translated and published by food historian and author Salma Yusuf Husain as a cookbook called *The Mughal Feast: Recipes from the Kitchen of Emperor Shah Jahan*. These recipes were designed to feed large numbers but offer plenty of insight into their flair, flavour and common ingredients. Nuts, all manner of fruits, saffron and decorative edible silver and gold leaves were abundant alongside common cooking techniques such as *dum pukht* – slow cooking over a flame in a pot sealed with dough – and *dhuni*, smoking food with charcoal. The use of sugar in savoury dishes was popular, but after trialling a few in my research I felt that this element of Mughal cuisine was just too sweet for the modern palate, and I have adjusted them accordingly. Despite their many iterations over the centuries, Mughal recipes retain echoes of their original glory that can be enjoyed in our twenty-first-century kitchens.

Haleem

Preparation time: 15 minutes
Cooking time: 1 hour
Serves 4-6

100g cracked or bulgur wheat

50g rolled oats

30g red split lentils (masoor)

30g white urid dal or black gram

30g yellow mung dal

2 tbsp basmati rice

1 tsp ground turmeric

1.3 litres cold water

2 heaped tbsp ghee

2 tbsp vegetable, sunflower or rapeseed oil

2 large white onions, finely sliced

1 heaped tsp finely grated garlic

1 tsp finely grated fresh ginger

500g chicken breasts, halved

1 fresh green chilli, finely chopped

1 tbsp haleem masala (see page 212)

500ml cold water

1 tsp fine salt, or to taste

Optional

1 tbsp ghee or vegetable, sunflower or rapeseed oil

1 tbsp julienned fresh ginger

2 dried whole red chillies

½ tbsp finely chopped fresh coriander leaves and stalks, to serve

1 tsp finely chopped fresh mint leaves, to serve

1 lemon, cut into wedges, to serve

This classic Mughal dish is both comforting and filling, sitting somewhere between a soup and a stew in consistency. It combines cracked or bulgur wheat, rolled oats and lentils with softened shredded meat – typically either beef, mutton or chicken. It was said to be introduced to the Northern Indian city of Hyderabad by the Arab diaspora during the reign of the sixth Nizam. Traditionally, a lot of ghee is used but I've gone for a more balanced approach between health and buttery decadence. The lentils and grains require 30 minutes soaking to aid digestion before cooking, and you'll need to make the quick haleem masala on page 212 before starting this recipe. This is a lovely dish for winter months when your body craves warming, nourishing food.

1. In a large mixing bowl, cover the cracked wheat, rolled oats, lentils and rice with cold water. Leave to soak for 1 to 2 hours, which helps with digestion and shortens the cooking time.

2. Drain the soaked ingredients and place them in a large pan. Add the ground turmeric and 1.3 litres of fresh water, then bring to the boil. Simmer gently for 30 minutes, skimming off any scum that forms on the surface.

3. You'll know the grains are cooked when they become mushier in consistency. Add a splash of water if it looks too thick or is beginning to stick to the bottom of the pan. Turn off the heat and then use a handheld blender to blend the mixture until smooth.

4. Meanwhile, heat the ghee and oil in a large pan and when hot, add the onions. Allow them to completely bronze and begin to crisp up over the next 15 to 20 minutes. Use a slotted spoon to remove the onions and place on kitchen paper to one side.

5. Using the same pan with a little more oil if required, cook the garlic and ginger, chicken pieces, fresh green chilli and haleem masala for 3 minutes before adding the 500ml of water to cover the chicken.

6. Simmer for 15 minutes, by which time the chicken will be cooked. Remove with a slotted spoon and then finely shred the chicken with two forks.

7. Pour the blended lentil mixture into the pan, then add the shredded chicken and half of the crispy onions back in. Mix well and continue to cook on a low heat for around 5 minutes. You are aiming for a thick porridge or *congee* consistency, as opposed to a thinner soup. Add the salt, adjust the seasoning to taste and then turn off the heat.

8. You can enjoy the haleem as is, but if you want to add a few toppings, first heat the ghee or oil in a small pan. Add the julienned ginger and dried chillies, stir for 10 seconds and then pour onto the haleem along with the remaining fried onions. Sprinkle with the fresh herbs and serve with lemon wedges.

Notes: If you want to make this gluten-free, you can leave out the cracked wheat, and if you don't have all three types of lentils you can just use one or two. You can replace the chicken with beef or lamb, but it will take longer to tenderise. To speed up this process, add ¾ tsp bicarbonate of soda to the raw meat and mix well. Leave for 15 minutes, then rinse under running water and pat dry before cooking. The cut of meat also affects how long it will take to cook and become tender – chuck beef, lamb shoulder or lamb neck are good options.

Haleem Masala

Preparation time: 5 minutes
Cooking time: 3 minutes
Makes 1 small pot

This masala takes minutes to prepare and stores in a sealed container for 3 months. It is required to make the comforting and filling dish haleem, which you can find on page 210.

5 cloves

2-inch piece of cinnamon or cassia bark

8 green cardamom pods, kept whole

2 black cardamom pods, seeds only

2 dried whole red chillies

1 tbsp coriander seeds

1 tbsp cumin seeds

1 tsp fennel seeds

1 tsp caraway seeds

1 tsp black peppercorns

1 tsp ground turmeric

½ tsp grated nutmeg

1. Heat a large frying pan and add all the ingredients except the turmeric and nutmeg. Move them around the pan for a minute, allowing the spices to awaken and release their aromas.

2. Pour the toasted spices into a large bowl and leave to cool before using a spice grinder or pestle and mortar to grind everything into a smooth powder.

3. Add the turmeric and nutmeg to the masala, then briefly blitz or stir again. Store in a sealed container, out of direct sunlight, for up to 3 months.

Spiced Greens with Quails' Eggs

Preparation time: 5 minutes
Cooking time: 10 minutes
Serves 2

2 tbsp vegetable, sunflower or rapeseed oil or ghee

¼ tsp asafoetida powder

1 tsp black or brown mustard seeds

1 dried whole red chilli, halved

½ onion, finely chopped

½ tsp fine salt

2 garlic cloves, finely chopped

1 tsp finely grated fresh ginger

½ tsp ground turmeric

½ tsp ground coriander

½ tsp Kashmiri chilli powder

400g greens such as spinach, chard or amaranth, washed and finely chopped

6-8 quail eggs

Wild game, including quail, was part of Mughal cuisine, so I wanted to create a Mughal-inspired recipe that focuses on quails' eggs. The Mughals often cooked with amaranth leaves, known as *chauli*, however this recipe works equally well with spinach or chard. It is great for breakfast, brunch or lunch and packed with lots of nutrients and a hint of spice.

1. Begin by heating the oil or ghee in a frying pan. When hot, add the asafoetida, mustard seeds and dried red chilli. Stir for 20 seconds before adding the onion and salt. Keep the heat medium to low.

2. Allow the onion to lightly bronze over the next 3 to 4 minutes before adding the garlic and ginger. After a minute, add the ground spices.

3. Stir everything to cook the spices before adding the greens. It is best to do this in batches, adding another batch once the first has wilted and softened. Mix well and simmer for a few minutes to cook off the water in the greens.

4. You can now choose to cook the quail eggs in one of two ways. Either lightly fry the eggs in a separate pan and then lay them on top of the spiced greens to serve, or make a well in the greens for each of your eggs with the back of a spoon, then crack an egg into each one. Cover the pan with a lid and leave the eggs to cook for a couple of minutes.

5. Serve immediately, being careful not to break up the eggs as you transfer them to plates along with the spiced greens.

Chicken Biryani Mughal Style

Preparation time: 20 minutes, plus 1-2 hours marinating
Cooking time: 1 hour 5 minutes
Serves 6

Step 1

1 heaped tbsp biryani masala (see page 218 or use store-bought)

1.3kg boneless chicken thighs, halved

2 tbsp fresh garlic and ginger paste

150g Greek yoghurt

1 lemon, juiced

1 tsp fine salt

Step 2

3 cloves

2 star anise

2 Indian bay leaves

10 fresh mint leaves

1 tbsp fresh coriander leaves

1 tsp caraway seeds

1 tbsp fine salt

400g long grain basmati rice, washed thoroughly with cold water

Step 3

6 tbsp vegetable, sunflower or rapeseed oil

4 large white onions, finely sliced

1 tsp fine salt

Step 4

Pinch of saffron threads, steeped in 4 tbsp warm milk

2 tbsp rose water

Step 5

2 small handfuls of fresh coriander, roughly chopped

2 small handfuls of fresh mint, roughly chopped

40g slivered almonds

40g cashew nuts

40g pistachios

30g raisins (optional)

6 tsp ghee

The exact origins of the biryani are often debated, but a clue may be in its Persian name, *birian*, meaning 'fried before cooking' and the word *birinj* which means rice. The royal courts of the Mughals adopted the biryani style of cooking and as the empire spread, so too did different techniques of preparing the dish. Today, India has a wide variety of biryani styles, each proclaiming to be superior! Some contain potatoes (Kolkata style), some use turmeric, some partially cook the meat and rice before layering while others cook everything together. This Mughal style biryani is opulent – with nuts, raisins and sweet-smelling rose water – yet very achievable at home. It uses the *dum* style of cooking, literally translated as 'to breathe' where food cooks gently in its own steam. The pot is traditionally sealed with dough, but foil is an easier modern alternative – either method allows the flavours to permeate and retain their fragrant perfection as the biryani cooks slowly over a heat source, traditionally a flame.

1. First, make your biryani masala, which takes minutes. The steps that follow are very easy, with crowd-pleasing results, so don't be put off by them!

2. In a large bowl, coat the chicken with all the ingredients for Step 1. Cover and leave in the fridge for 1 to 2 hours. When ready to cook, bring the chicken to room temperature.

3. Heat a large pan of water and add all the Step 2 ingredients except the rice. Once boiling, add the rice. Turn the heat down, cover and cook for 6 minutes. The rice should be partially cooked (around 60%) so that it retains some bite.

4. Remove the cloves, star anise, bay, coriander and mint leaves with a slotted spoon (leaving the caraway seeds) and then drain the rice and briefly run under cold water. Spread the rice out evenly on a large baking tray to cool.

5. In a large cast-iron pan, heat the oil in Step 3. Add the onions and salt. Allow to bronze and crisp up for around 15 minutes, then remove half the onions and place on kitchen paper to absorb excess oil.

6. Add a little more oil if required, then add the marinated chicken to the pan. Keep on a low heat and cook for 20 minutes, turning the chicken intermittently. Now turn off the heat and remove half the chicken.

7. Spread half the cooled rice on top of the chicken in the pan. Add half the ingredients of Steps 4 and 5, scattering them evenly over the rice.

8. Add the second layer of chicken back to the pan, followed by the remaining rice and Step 4 and 5 ingredients. Scatter with the reserved crispy onions.

9. Cover the pan tightly with tin foil and secure it with the lid. Cook over a low heat for 20 minutes, then turn off the heat and leave covered for a further 15 minutes. You can also cook this in a preheated oven at 180°C/160°C fan/350°F/Gas 4 for 20 minutes, then take it out and rest without removing the lid for 15 minutes.

10. Serve your biryani with raita, sliced raw red onion and a boiled egg per serving.

Notes: To seal the pan with dough, mix white or wholewheat flour with a pinch of salt and water, roll out and seal over the pan by pinching the edges.

Biryani Masala

Preparation time: 5 minutes
Cooking time: 2 minutes
Makes 1 small pot

2 tbsp coriander seeds

1½ tbsp cumin seeds

1½ tsp caraway seeds

1 tbsp fennel seeds

1 tbsp black peppercorns

1 tbsp green cardamom pods

8 black cardamom pods

2 mace blades

1 whole nutmeg

½ tbsp cloves

3 star anise

3 dried whole red chillies (optional)

4 Indian bay leaves (see notes)

Homemade masalas take no time to rustle up and completely elevate a dish. Of course, if you don't have or can't find all the individual spices listed below you can purchase store-bought blends instead. The whole spices are first dry roasted before being ground into a fine powder. This masala has warming aromatic notes that infuse the biryani on page 216.

1. Heat a large frying pan and add the first 5 ingredients (seeds and peppercorns). Move them around the pan for 30 seconds before adding all the remaining ingredients.

2. Use a spatula to continue moving the spices around the pan. Heating them up awakens the spices to release their oils and aromas, which will enhance your masala, so don't skip this step!

3. After 90 seconds, pour the spices into a bowl and allow to cool before placing into a spice grinder. Blitz to a smooth powder.

4. Store the masala in a sealed container and use over the next 3 months.

Notes: Caraway seeds are also known as *shahjeera* or black cumin. They have a different, more mildly sweet flavour profile to cumin. If you can't find Indian bay leaves, also known as *tej patta*, leave them out altogether. European bay has a very different flavour profile.

Keema Samosa

Preparation time: 30 minutes
Cooking time: 45 minutes
Makes 20

1 tbsp rose water

Pinch of saffron threads

3 tbsp vegetable, sunflower or rapeseed oil

1 tbsp finely grated fresh ginger

1 tbsp finely grated garlic

1 aubergine, grated

200g (approx. 2 large) large onions, puréed

1 tsp fine salt

500g minced lamb

1 tsp caster sugar

270g filo pastry sheets

3 tbsp water

1-2 eggs, whisked

Nestled within the British Library in London is *The Sultan's Book of Delights* – a fifteenth-century book of recipes from the Sultan of Mandu (Madhya Pradesh), known as *Ghiyath Shahi*, and later added to by his son and successor Nasir Shah. It is also known more formally as the *Ni'matnāma-i-Nāṣir al-Dīn Shāhī*. Beautiful miniature illustrations of dishes being prepared sit alongside handwritten notes, observations and recipes. Exact measurements are often omitted, leaving it to the reader to guess the proportions. Within its pages, the ingredients for samosas are included, from which I've created my own version of Mughal samosas. Traditionally, they were deep-fried but I've opted to bake them, a healthier and equally delicious method of preparing them in your home kitchen.

1.   Begin by placing the rose water and saffron in a small bowl. Gently mix well with a teaspoon and set aside.

2.   Heat the oil in a frying pan on a medium to low heat and then add the ginger and garlic. Stir for 1 minute before adding the grated aubergine.

3.   After 3 to 4 minutes, add the onion purée and salt and let this bronze over the next 8 to 10 minutes, stirring intermittently to avoid it catching on the bottom of the pan. Add more oil as required.

4.   Next, add the minced lamb and stir into the aubergine, onion, garlic and ginger. Simmer gently for 10 minutes and then add the rose water, saffron threads and sugar. Simmer for a further 5 minutes and then taste to check the seasoning. Set aside to cool.

5.   Place the filo pastry on a clean surface and cut into three equal parts lengthways. Cover it all with a damp tea towel to stop the filo drying out.

6.   Taking one strip of filo pastry, lay it out vertically. Take the bottom right-hand corner and fold up to the left edge to create a triangle. Fold it over again to the opposite edge, creating another, smaller triangle. Do this once more, back to the left edge, and you will have created a little pocket or cone with a strip of pastry left at the top.

7.   Fill the pocket with 2 to 3 teaspoons of the cooled filling. Now continue folding the pocket in the same way as you did to begin with to form triangles. Do this until you run out of pastry.

8.   Dip your finger in the water and run it along the top edge of the pastry, pressing gently to help seal the samosa. Use a pastry brush to brush the samosa all over with egg wash and place on a lined baking tray.

9.   Continue with Steps 6 to 8 until the rest of the pastry strips and the filling have been used up.

10. Bake the samosas in a preheated oven at 200°C/180°C fan/400°F/Gas 6 for 15 minutes. Serve hot and enjoy.

Notes: You can make this with beef or chicken mince instead of lamb, or paneer for vegetarian samosas, or tofu for a vegan alternative. If you want to make the samosas in advance, they can be frozen after Step 8 and then brushed again with egg wash before being cooked from frozen.

Hara Bhara Kebabs

Preparation time: 10 minutes
Cooking time: 50 minutes
Makes 22

2 large potatoes (360g)

5 tbsp vegetable, sunflower or rapeseed oil

2 fresh green chillies, slit lengthways

1 tsp cumin seeds

1 tbsp ginger-garlic paste

200g green beans, fresh or frozen

200g frozen peas

250g fresh spinach, washed

40g fresh coriander

1 tsp fine salt

1 tsp chat masala powder

½ tsp garam masala

5 tbsp fine breadcrumbs

These delicately spiced green vegetable patties are deliciously moreish. The kebab itself is of Arabic origin and was used to describe roasted meats. They were first introduced to India during the Mughal rule and are now widely eaten across the world. I first came across these crispy patties not in India but in the hugely popular Indian snack shop in Tooting known as Pooja. I often stop by during my spice tours to pick up some delicious snacks, but the kebabs are only on offer at the weekends when they are made fresh. They are vegan and packed full of green vegetables, great as a pre-dinner snack.

1. Without peeling them, place the potatoes in a pan of boiling water and cook for up to 30 minutes until soft, depending on the size of the potatoes you are using. Test with a sharp knife to check they are cooked through before removing from the pan and setting aside to cool. Once cooled, remove the skins and then mash the potatoes.

2. Heat 2 tablespoons of the oil in a large frying pan, then add the fresh green chillies, cumin seeds and ginger-garlic paste. Stir for 20 seconds before adding the green beans, peas, spinach and coriander. Season with salt, place a lid on the pan and stir intermittently until the vegetables have completely softened. This will take around 8 minutes.

3. Transfer the contents of the pan to a blender and blitz. You may have to do this in two batches. Add the mashed potato to the blender and blitz again to combine everything, then turn out into a mixing bowl.

4. Add the chat masala, garam masala and breadcrumbs to the potato mixture and mix well. Taste to check the salt levels and add more if required.

5. Rub a little oil on your hands and take a golf ball sized piece of the mixture, rolling it into a sphere and then gently flattening to form a small patty, no larger than 2.5 inches across. Place on an oiled plate (to stop them sticking) and repeat until all the mixture has been used. They are delicate so take your time to prepare these kebabs.

6. Coat the bottom of a frying pan with some of the remaining oil, place on a medium high heat and add the patties. I suggest doing this in batches so as not to overcrowd the pan. Keep the heat on medium to high so that the patties bronze and crisp up, which should take around 2 to 3 minutes on each side. Once they have bronzed on both sides, remove from the pan and place on kitchen paper while you make the rest.

7. You can make these ahead of time and then reheat in the oven or enjoy them at room temperature, although personally I like to eat them warm.

Notes: These kebabs are really delicate so they need to be handled with care. They do firm up slightly as they begin to cool but they're best eaten just after cooking.

Coconut Shorba

Preparation time: 15 minutes
Cooking time: 15 minutes
Serves 4

2 tbsp vegetable, sunflower or coconut oil

1 tsp fennel seeds

2 large white onions, finely chopped

1 tsp fine salt

1 large carrot, finely chopped

2-inch piece (30g) of fresh ginger, finely grated or chopped

1-2 fresh green chillies, roughly chopped (deseeded for less heat)

400ml tin of full-fat coconut milk

500ml water

1 lime, juiced

Handful of fresh coriander, roughly chopped including stalks

Freshly ground black pepper, to serve

Typically, Mughlai cuisine is thought of as rich, decadent, robust and often meaty. Emperor Aurangzeb, the Mughal ruler from 1658 to 1707, was a devout vegetarian for most of his life, however. *Shorbas* (soups) were widely consumed during his rule as a light yet comforting vegetarian meal. This recipe is believed to have originated from the valley of Peshawar, historically known as the Gandhara valley, located in what is now Pakistan. Quick to prepare and deliciously nourishing, I have adapted it slightly to include fennel seeds for a delicate aroma. This is great as a starter or light lunch, served with some crusty bread.

1. Begin by heating the oil in a medium pan. Add the fennel seeds, followed by the onions and salt. Lightly cook for 4 minutes until the raw smell has dissipated and the onion is translucent.

2. Add the carrot, ginger and fresh green chillies. Stir for a minute before adding the tin of coconut milk and the water. Allow to simmer on a low heat for 6 to 8 minutes, by which time the carrot will have softened.

3. Add the lime juice and fresh coriander, then immediately blitz the soup with a handheld blender until smooth. You can then strain it for a thinner and smoother consistency if you like, or eat as is, topped with some freshly ground black pepper.

Mughlai Green Moong Dal

Preparation time: 6 hours or overnight
Cooking time: I hour 20 minutes
Serves 4-6

250g whole green moong/mung dal

1.3 litres water

2 black cardamom pods

I Indian bay leaf (optional)

2-inch piece of cinnamon or cassia bark

2-3 tbsp vegetable, sunflower or rapeseed oil

2 large white onions, finely sliced

For the tempering ingredients

I-2 tbsp vegetable, sunflower or rapeseed oil

I tsp cumin seeds

I fresh green chilli, finely chopped (optional)

I large white onion, finely chopped

I tsp fine salt

4 garlic cloves, finely chopped

I-inch piece (15g) of fresh ginger, finely chopped

I heaped tsp ground coriander

½ tsp Kashmiri chilli powder

½ tsp freshly ground black pepper

150ml yoghurt

To serve

I tsp butter or ghee per portion

50ml fresh cream (optional)

This dal is a hug in a bowl and very filling. Not to be confused with dal makhani, it uses the whole green moong, also known as green mung, which require soaking. Typically, I soak them overnight or for at least 6 hours, so it does require a little forward planning. The cooking stage is very straightforward, and the dal lasts in the fridge for 5 days or can be frozen. It's a decadent and rich meal thanks to the addition of fried onion, yoghurt, ghee and cream – perfect for a Mughal banquet. It can also be made dairy-free if you wish – see the notes below.

1. Place the green moong dal in a large mixing bowl and cover with cold water. Leave to soak for 6 hours or overnight.

2. After soaking, drain the green moong dal and then place in a large deep pan and cover with the 1.3 litres of fresh water. Add the black cardamom, Indian bay leaf and cinnamon or cassia bark and simmer for 45 to 50 minutes, by which time the dal should be soft when pressed between your thumb and forefinger.

3. Meanwhile, heat the oil in a medium pan and add the onions. Fry on a low heat for 15 minutes or until bronzed, then remove with a slotted spoon and place on kitchen paper to soak up excess oil.

4. Use the same pan for the tempering ingredients. Add the oil and when hot, add the cumin seeds and fresh green chilli, if using. Stir for 20 seconds, then add the onion and salt. Allow this to lightly bronze for 4 to 5 minutes and then add the garlic and ginger.

5. After a couple of minutes, add the ground spices with a drop of water to stop them from burning and simmer gently for a couple of minutes.

6. Now turn the heat right down and add the yoghurt. Mix well and continue to simmer on a low heat.

7. Break up the crispy fried onions from Step 3 with your hands and place half into the spiced onion and yoghurt mixture. Mix well and then pour the contents of this pan into the pan of green moong dal.

8. Add some more water if the dal looks a little thick and simmer gently for 10 minutes to allow all the flavours to infuse. Taste to check the seasoning and add more salt if required.

9. Just before serving, turn off the heat and scatter the remaining crispy onions over the dal. If using, drizzle the cream and butter or ghee on top, then enjoy with steamed basmati rice.

Notes: To make this dal dairy-free, omit the yoghurt, butter/ghee and cream. In Step 6, add 2 large tomatoes, blended to a purée, to the tempering ingredients instead of the yoghurt.

Lamb Pasanda

Preparation time: 25 minutes
Cooking time: 1 hour
Serves 4-6

1kg lamb neck, thinly sliced (approx. 2.5 x 0.5 inches)

½ tsp Kashmiri chilli powder

1 tsp ground turmeric

1 tsp fine salt

4 tbsp vegetable, sunflower or rapeseed oil

2 white onions, finely sliced

1 tbsp ghee (optional)

1 tbsp finely grated fresh ginger

1 tbsp finely grated garlic

1 tsp ground coriander

1 tsp fine sugar

100ml water

300g full-fat natural or Greek yoghurt (or a dairy-free alternative such as Alpro Plain)

1 tbsp slivered almonds, to serve

Fresh coriander, to serve

For the pasanda masala

15 whole almonds

5 cloves

5 black peppercorns

5 green cardamom pods, seeds only

1 black cardamom pod, seeds only

1-inch piece of cinnamon or cassia bark

1 tbsp white poppy seeds

1 tsp cumin seeds

This was a favoured dish in the courts of the Mughal emperors – the word *pasande* means favourite in Urdu. Only the best cuts of lamb or goat were used, and the preparation of the meat is important too – it needs to be sliced thinly into small strips, as opposed to chunks or cubes. If you have bought cubed lamb, simply place some baking parchment over it on a flat surface and then use a rolling pin to bash the lamb a few times so that it tenderises and flattens. Pasanda is a very mellow and lightly spiced dish, similar to a korma, and great for all the family.

1. Begin by toasting all the pasanda masala ingredients in a dry frying pan on a medium to high heat for a minute. Move them around the pan continuously to avoid burning, then transfer to a small bowl to cool.

2. Using a spice grinder or pestle and mortar, grind the cooled masala ingredients to a powder.

3. Place the lamb in a bowl and coat thoroughly with the pasanda masala, Kashmiri chilli powder and ground turmeric. Cover and place in the fridge. You can do this the day before cooking and leave the lamb to marinate overnight, or you can continue straight to the next step if you are short of time.

4. Add half the oil to a pan and then add the onions. Cook on a medium-low heat for 10 to 15 minutes until bronzed, stirring intermittently. Remove and place on kitchen paper to soak up excess oil and then place in a wet grinder to form a smooth paste.

5. Add the ghee, if using, and remaining oil to the same pan on a medium-low heat. Add the grated garlic and ginger, stir for a minute and then add the marinated lamb. Move everything around the pan intermittently to stop it catching on the bottom.

6. After 5 minutes, lower the heat and add the ground coriander, sugar, yoghurt and fried onion paste. Mix well and continue to cook, then after 5 minutes, add the water and cover the pan.

7. Leave the pasanda to simmer, stirring intermittently, for 30 minutes. If it becomes too thick, simply add a little more water. Alternatively, you can cook the pasanda in a preheated oven at 180°C/160°C fan/350°F/Gas 4 for 30 minutes.

8. Serve with a scattering of slivered almonds and fresh coriander alongside plain basmati rice or the Parsi 'Brown' Rice on page 186.

Masala Omelette Mughal Style

Preparation time: 10 minutes
Cooking time: 10 minutes
Serves 2

Pinch of saffron threads

Pinch of ground cloves

Pinch of ground cinnamon

Pinch of ground green cardamom, or crushed seeds from 1 green cardamom pod

½ tsp finely crushed black peppercorns

4 eggs

½ small red or white onion, finely chopped

1-inch piece (15g) of fresh ginger, finely grated

Handful of fresh coriander, finely chopped

1 tsp fine salt

1 tbsp butter or ghee

This recipe differs from a regular masala omelette in that it doesn't contain tomatoes, cumin seeds or even ground turmeric. Instead, a delicate fine powder of cinnamon, cloves, green cardamom and black pepper introduces a sweet note alongside the savoury flavours of the onions, ginger, fresh coriander and eggs. This recipe is adapted from the *khagina-e-baize* in Salma Yusuf Husain's book *The Mughal Feast* which is in turn a translation of an original handwritten Persian recipe book called *Nuskha-e-Shahjahani*. My version is quick to rustle up and really hits the spot.

1. Drop the saffron into a few tablespoons of warm water in a small bowl. Combine the remaining spices – cloves, cinnamon, cardamom and peppercorns – in a separate bowl.

2. Crack the eggs into another, larger bowl and whisk well. Add the onion, ginger, fresh coriander and salt. Mix well, then add the spice masala.

3. Heat half the butter or ghee in a medium frying pan and then add half the spiced egg mixture and cook on a medium-low heat for 2 minutes. Check to see if the omelette is nicely bronzing on the bottom and then gently turn it over and cook for a further 1 to 2 minutes.

4. Transfer the omelette to a warm plate and drizzle a teaspoon of the saffron water over the top. Repeat with the second omelette.

Nihari

Preparation time: 20 minutes

Cooking time: 1-2 hours

Serves 6

2 tbsp vegetable, sunflower or rapeseed oil

2 tbsp ghee or butter (optional)

2 large white onions, thinly sliced

1 tsp fine salt

1 tbsp finely grated garlic

1 tbsp finely grated fresh ginger

1.2kg meat of your choice, on the bone (such as beef shank, lamb neck or shoulder, chicken legs and thighs)

1 portion of nihari masala (see page 234)

800ml water

3 tbsp plain or chickpea/gram flour

1 tbsp chopped fresh coriander

1 tbsp fresh ginger batons

Nihari is a very straightforward dish to make, although it does take time to cook. You can make it on the hob or in the oven, pressure cooker or slow cooker. The masala takes minutes to prepare and although it does require a range of spices, they are worth investing in and used on repeat throughout this book. Nihari comes from Lucknow and can be made with beef, lamb or chicken. Take your pick! On the bone is best as the meat will fall off it easily and provide heaps of flavour, but boneless cuts will be delicious too.

1. Begin by making the nihari masala on page 234.

2. In a large cast-iron pot, heat the oil and ghee or butter if using. Add the onions and salt, then allow to lightly bronze over the next 6 to 8 minutes on a medium-low heat.

3. Next add the garlic and ginger, stir for 3 minutes, then increase the heat and add the meat. Sear on all sides for 3 to 4 minutes before lowering the heat.

4. Stir the nihari masala into the meat and onions, making sure it's well mixed, then pour in the water which should be enough to cover the meat.

5. Place a lid on the pan and cook gently for 40 to 50 minutes if using chicken, 1 hour for lamb and 1 hour 30 minutes for beef, or longer as required for the meat to be completely tender. If you are cooking this in the oven, it should be preheated to 200°C/180°C fan/400°F/Gas 6.

6. Mix the flour with a little cold water to create a paste, then stir this into the nihari to help thicken the gravy. Cook for a further 10 to 20 minutes.

7. Taste to check the salt levels and add a little more if required. When you're happy with the flavours, serve with the fresh coriander and ginger batons scattered on top.

Notes: Eat this with the Sheermal on page 238 to mop up all those juices. It's great made in advance and freezes well.

Nihari Masala

Preparation time: 5 minutes
Cooking time: 3 minutes
Makes 1 portion

6 green cardamom pods

2 black cardamom pods

5 cloves

2 Indian bay leaves

3 long peppers

1 mace blade

1 star anise

2-inch piece of cinnamon or cassia bark

1 tbsp fennel seeds

1 tbsp coriander seeds

1 tsp caraway seeds

1 tsp cumin seeds

1 tsp black peppercorns

½ tsp ground nutmeg, or a small piece of whole nutmeg

1 tsp ground turmeric

2 tsp ground ginger

2 tsp Kashmiri chilli powder

This masala is integral when making the splendid Mughal dish of the same name, which comes from the Arabic word nahaar meaning morning. While it does include a number of whole spices which are then ground, I hope that the spice enthusiasts among you might already have many of these and will easily be able to source the others easily at an Asian grocer or online.

1. Heat a large frying pan on a low heat and add all the whole spices, leaving the ground nutmeg, turmeric, ginger and Kashmiri chilli powder to one side.

2. Move everything around the pan for a couple of minutes, allowing the aromatics to awaken without burning.

3. Transfer the spices into a large bowl to cool, then blend in a spice grinder until you have a fine powder. Return this powder to the large bowl, add the ground spices and mix well.

4. Store the masala in a sealed glass jar until ready to use.

Notes: Long pepper, or *piper longum* as it is also known, can easily be sourced online or in Asian grocers. It is slightly hotter than a black pepper with notes of nutmeg and clove. It grew wild in East Bengal and was regarded as the go-to heat-giving spice in India long before the chilli was introduced by the Portuguese.

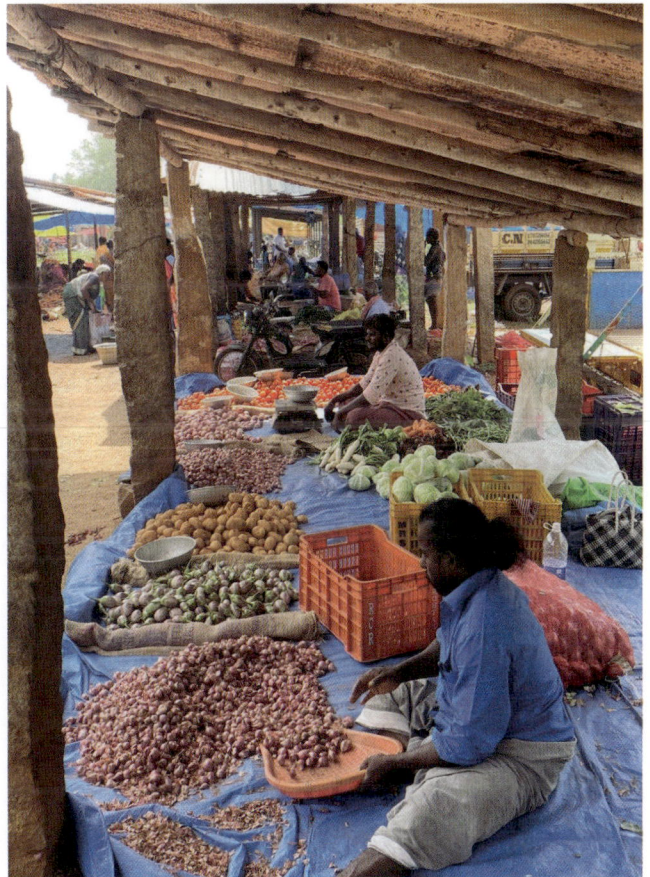

Shami Kebabs

Preparation time: 20 minutes
Cooking time: 12-15 minutes
Makes 16

500g lamb, beef or chicken mince

1 onion, finely chopped

1-inch piece (15g) of ginger, finely grated

3 tsp coriander seeds, roughly crushed

2 tsp fennel seeds, roughly crushed

1 egg

1 tbsp full-fat yoghurt, strained

3 tbsp chickpea/gram flour

1 tsp fine salt

2-inch piece of cinnamon or cassia bark

4 green cardamom pods, kept whole

1 black cardamom pod, kept whole

1 tsp black peppercorns

5 cloves

2-3 tbsp olive oil

These smooth round patties, made with beef, lamb or chicken mince, were a favourite in the royal Mughal courts. Legend has it they were created for a toothless *Nawab* (nobleman) in Lucknow, as the patties are so soft that he was able to eat them.

1. Begin by placing your mince into a blender along with the onion, ginger, crushed coriander and fennel seeds, egg, strained yoghurt, flour and salt. Pulse briefly to combine all the ingredients.

2. Finely grind the cinnamon or cassia bark, cardamom pods, black peppercorns and cloves in a spice grinder or pestle and mortar to form a smooth powder.

3. Add the spice powder to the mince and mix well. Rub a little oil over your hands and shape the mince mixture into round, evenly sized patties about 2 inches wide and no more than 1 inch thick.

4. Heat the olive oil in a large frying pan and shallow fry the patties on a medium heat until bronzed on both sides. This should take 5 to 6 minutes in total, and I recommend cooking them in batches so you don't overcrowd the pan. Place the cooked patties on kitchen paper to soak up excess oil.

5. Serve the patties warm with the Himalayan Hot Sauce on page 176, alongside Allegra's Kachumber Salad (see page 76).

Notes: The Mughals often steamed or smoked their food, known as the *dum* and *dhuni* methods respectively. To smoke these patties, a small heatproof bowl would be placed in the centre of a large pan or pot, surrounded by the uncooked patties. An onion skin and a hot coal would be placed in the bowl, ghee poured over it and a lid quickly secured on top to stop the smoke escaping. The small bowl with the hot coal and onion skin would then be removed and discarded, leaving the patties with a wonderful smoked flavour after cooking.

Sheermal

Preparation time: 2 hours
Cooking time: 20 minutes
Makes 6

300g bread flour or plain flour

1 tbsp caster sugar (optional)

1 tsp easy bake/instant yeast

1 tsp fine salt

½ tsp ground cardamom

40ml melted ghee or neutral oil

160ml warm milk

1 tsp rose essence

¼ tsp saffron threads

Extra melted ghee, to brush before serving

These soft, lightly sweetened, pillowy flatbreads were a favourite of the *Nawabs* (nobility) during the Mughal era. Originating from Iran, in Persian the word sheermal means 'milk rubbed'. They were and continue to be hugely popular in Lucknow, Hyderabad and Kashmir. Saffron is the star ingredient in this recipe, and sometimes cardamom is also included. Often eaten alongside a mutton nihari, korma or vegetable curry, they are perfect for mopping up sauces.

1. Combine the flour, sugar if using, yeast, salt and ground cardamom in a bowl. Next, add the melted ghee or oil, 140ml of the warm milk and the rose essence.

2. Combine the ingredients to form a soft dough, either by hand or in a stand mixer with a dough hook on a low speed for 5 minutes. Knead for the same amount of time and then return to the bowl and cover with a damp tea towel or clingfilm and set aside in a warm place to prove, ideally for around 90 minutes (see notes).

3. Cut the proved dough into 6 equal portions and roll out each portion into a thin disc, no larger than 5 inches in diameter.

4. Use a fork to prick the surface of the dough. You can keep the sheermal plain or top them with slivered almonds, pistachios or sesame seed at this stage, pressing any toppings firmly in place.

5. Place the saffron into a small bowl with the remaining 20ml of warm milk. Mix well and leave to steep for 15 minutes, by which time the milk will have taken on a lovely yellow colour.

6. Preheat your oven to 200°C/180°C fan/400°F/Gas 6. Place the breads on a baking tray lined with baking paper and brush with the saffron milk. Bake for 13 to 15 minutes, by which time the sheermal should be lightly bronzed.

7. Finally, lightly brush the hot sheermal with melted ghee and then serve immediately.

Notes: If you prefer to use active dry yeast, you need to activate it before use with a teaspoon of sugar and a little warm (not hot!) water. Combine in a small bowl and leave for 10 minutes.

When proving dough, I always pop the oven on a low heat for 5 minutes and then turn it off completely, keeping the oven door slightly ajar and the light switched on. I then place the covered bowl of dough in the warm oven to prove until it rises. If you live in a warm climate, simply leave the covered dough to one side and it will prove at room temperature.

You can store the cooked sheermal for a few days by wrapping them in foil and placing in an airtight container. Reheat them in an oven when you are ready to eat. They can also be frozen after Step 6 and reheated from frozen on a dry tawa or frying pan (do not add any oil) to thaw and lightly bronze on each side before being brushed with ghee and served.

Menu Ideas

When cooking from this book you can absolutely pick a recipe from one chapter and eat it with any dish from another. There are no set rules or restrictions here; explore the dishes and weave your own favourites into your culinary repertoire. Below is a rough guide to start you off, from everyday occasions to something a little more special.

Midweek Suppers

Chicken Curry Himalayan Style

Chicken Stew

Coconut Shorba

Fish Ball Soup

Fruity Meat Glassy

Hakka Chilli Paneer

Kallappam – Rice Pancake

Nepali Mixed Lentil Stew

Phingsha – Chicken with Glass Noodles

Sichuan Fried Rice

Sweet and Sour Prawn Patio

Tangy Fish Curry

Afternoon Tea

Banana and Cinnamon Fritters

Coconut Pancakes

Hara Bhara Kebabs

Keema Samosa

Red Bean Sesame Balls

Ricotta and Cardamom Teacake

Rissois de Camarão – Prawn Patties

Shami Kebabs

Shaphalay

Sweetly Spiced Rice Flakes

Make Ahead

Biryani Masala

Chicken Momo

Haleem Masala

Hara Bara Kebabs

Himalayan Hot Sauce

Keema Samosa

Keralan Garam Masala

Madras Curry Powder

Mango Chutney

Parsi Sambar Masala

Prawn Balchão

Recheado Masala

Rissois de Camarão – Prawn Patties

Savoury Steamed Buns

Shaphalay

Sheermal

Sichuan Chilli Sauce

Tibetan Steamed Buns

Vegan

Bamboo Shoot and Potato Curry

Black Chickpea Curry

Chana Ros

Country Captain Vegetables

Gobi Manchurian

Manchow Soup

Mori Dar

Mughlai Green Moong Dal

Nepali Mixed Lentil Stew

Parsi Sweet and Sour Vegetable Stew

Potato Bhaji

Pumpkin and Tamarind Soup

Pumpkin Vindaloo

Sichuan Chilli Honey Roasties

Sikkim Nettle Soup

Stuffed Aubergines with Recheado Masala

Sweetcorn Soup with Chilli Vinegar

Tibetan Steamed Buns

Vegetable Thukpa

On a Budget

Aloo Dum

Anglo-Indian Mulligatawny

Chicken Korma

Country Captain Vegetables

Eggs on Okra

Fish Ball Soup

Fruity Meat Glassy

Kallappam – Rice Pancake

Kedgeree

Manchow Soup

Masala Omelette Mughal Style

Mori Dar

Pish Pash

Pumpkin and Tamarind Soup

Shami Kebabs

Spiced Cassava

Tibetan Steamed Buns

Vegetable Dhansak

Veggie Hakka Noodles

Leisurely Weekends

Chicken Momo

Chilli Chicken

Coconut Shorba

Goan Frijoada

Gobi Manchurian

Haleem

Jardaloo Salli Boti

Kedgeree

Manchow Soup

Nihari

Parsi 'Brown' Rice

Prawn Cutlets

Railway Lamb Curry

Runner Beans with Lamb

Savoury Steamed Buns

Shami Kebabs

Sheermal

Sichuan Chilli Honey Roasties

Sichuan Fried Rice

Stuffed Aubergine Cutlets

Sweet and Sour Vegetable Stew

Sweetened Lamb Pulao

Tangy Fish Curry

Whole Fish Pollichathu

Light Meals and Speedy Lunches

Anglo-Indian Mulligatawny

Bamboo Shoot and Potato Curry

Black Chickpea Curry

Chana Ros

Eggs on Okra

Fish Ball Soup

Hakka Chilli Paneer

Hara Bhara Kebabs

Kallappam – Rice Pancake

Kedgeree

Manchow Soup

Masala Omelette Mughal Style

Mulligatawny Parsi Style

Pish Pash

Potato Bhaji

Prawn Fry

Prawn Peera

Pumpkin and Tamarind Soup

Shaptak – Tibetan Stir Fry

Sichuan Fried Rice

Sikkim Nettle Soup

Spiced Greens with Quail's Eggs

Sweet and Sour Prawn Patio

Sweetcorn Soup with Chilli Vinegar

Vegetable Thukpa

Dinner Parties for 4-8

If you are cooking for 8 people and the recipe serves 4-6, simply add an extra 200g of the main protein, keeping all other proportions the same. Typically, I would cook one meat or fish dish, two vegetable curries, a dal and a spiced rice for a dinner party of this size. I might also start with a snack like the keema samosa or shaphalay with some Himalayan hot sauce on the side, before guests sit down to the meal.

Bamboo Shoot and Potato Curry

Chana Ros

Chicken Biryani

Chicken Cafreal

Chicken Korma

Chicken Stew

Chicken Xacuti

Chilli Chicken

Duck Roast

Goan Frijoada

Goan Pork Sorpotel

Hakka Chilli Paneer

Jardaloo Salli Boti

Keema Samosa

Keralan Beef Fry

Lamb Pasanda

Mori Dar

Mughlai Green Moong Dal

Nepali Mixed Lentil Stew

Nihari

Parsi 'Brown' Rice

Pork Vindaloo

Prawn Fry

Railway Lamb Curry

Runner Beans with Lamb

Sichuan Chilli Honey Roasties

Sichuan Fried Rice

Sweet and Sour Vegetable Stew

Sweetcorn Soup with Chilli Vinegar

Whole Fish Pollichathu

Sample Menus

I often start with soup, dal, momo, steamed buns, patties, kebabs or shaphalay before moving onto the main dishes. Simply skip these snacks if you want a lighter meal and include or omit a sweet treat to finish, depending on your preference and appetite.

Option 1

Sweetcorn Soup with Chilli Vinegar

Chicken Biryani or Kedgeree

Allegra's Kachumber Salad

Red Bean Sesame Balls

Option 2

Pumpkin and Tamarind Soup

Duck Roast or Jardaloo Salli Boti

Arroz Pulao or Parsi Brown Rice

Nepali Mixed Lentil Stew

Wedding Pickle

Option 3

Rissois de Camarão

Mori Dar

Chicken Cafreal or Goan Frijoada

Allegra's Kachumber Salad

Parsi Brown Rice or Arroz Pulao

Coconut Pancakes

Option 4

Chicken Momo or Vegetable Momo with Chilli Oil

Gobi Manchurian or Chilli Chicken

Sichuan Fried Rice

Potato Bhaji

Option 5

Fish Ball Soup

Tibetan Steamed Buns with Himalayan Hot Sauce

Hakka Chilli Paneer

Banana and Cinnamon Fritters

Option 6

Manchow Soup

Keralan Beef Fry or Fruity Meat Glassy

Country Captain Vegetables

Mango Chutney

Sheermal or Arroz Pulao

Option 7

Coconut Shorba with Chilli Oil

Phingsha or Veggie Hakka Noodles

Red Bean Sesame Balls

Spice Suppliers

Living in London, I'm in the fortunate position of being able to source spices and fresh herbs very easily. For those in a more rural setting who may not have the same access, I thought it would be helpful to list a few of my favourite suppliers who are able to send you ingredients that may not be available from your local supermarket or farmers' market. If these suppliers don't have the product you are after, the usual online giant probably will, but please try these small family-run businesses first.

UK Suppliers

Sous Chef

An independent family company focused on handpicking the best products from the world's kitchens. As well as an incredible range of ingredients they also sell tableware, cookware and gifts. Ingredients in my book that may seem trickier to get hold of, such as Sichuan pepper, black fungus, Chinkiang black rice vinegar and Bengali five spice can all be purchased here.

www.souschef.co.uk

Spice Mountain

Launched by Magali and her partner Matt, this company is a true spice emporium. They source every spice you could possibly want so are a great place to visit online or in person at their Aladdin's cave of a store in Borough Market.

www.spicemountain.co.uk
Borough Market, 8 Southwark Street, London, SE1 1TL

Ottolenghi

An online pantry for a wide range of ingredients that can sometimes be tricky to source.

www.ottolenghi.co.uk

The Spice Shop

Based in Notting Hill and Brighton, this independent family-run business is also able to send spices and fresh curry leaves to you. Their London shop is opposite the famous Books for Cooks and if you visit around lunchtime, you may be able to secure a spot there for a bite to eat, as the bookshop transforms into a café with food cooked by the owner, Eric, and staff from a different recipe book each day.

www.thespiceshop.co.uk
1 Blenheim Crescent, London, W11 2EE
10 Gardner Street, Brighton, BN1 1UP

Patel Brothers

Established over four decades ago, the younger generation have taken the reins of this family-run business. They stock a wide range of spices and Indian produce, including fresh curry leaves. Much of this can be bought in their online shop too but if you are in Tooting do pay them a visit and mention my name! They are always happy to help you source the spice you need. (Another store, Bhavin's Food, is just a few doors down which has a huge range of fresh produce and is worth a visit too.)

www.asiandukan.co.uk
187-189 Upper Tooting Road, London, SW17 7TG

US Suppliers

Kalustyan's

If you are based state-side, Kalustyan's on Lexington Avenue in Manhattan, New York City, is a landmark for global spices. Set up in 1944, this intimate neighbourhood shop is a must-visit for seasoned chefs and adventurous home cooks. They deliver nationwide in the US.

www.foodsofnations.com
123 Lexington Avenue, New York, NY 10016

Burlap & Barrel

Set up in 2016 by Ethan and Ori, Burlap & Barrel offer magnificent, sustainably sourced, single-origin spices. They are beautifully packaged too, so make a great gift. They only deliver to the US and Canada.

www.burlapandbarrel.com

SOS Chef

A well-curated and highly-regarded herbs and spices shop that is a favourite among passionate home cooks and chefs alike. A great place to explore and pick up some pantry staples as well as more unusual spices.

www.sos-chefs.com
104 Avenue B, New York, NY 10009

The Spice House

Founded in 1957, this company has an excellent range of spices, herbs and blends. You can visit them online or find their products in physical stores across the US. See their website for locations and more info.

www.thespicehouse.com

Australian Suppliers

Aussie Spices Online

This company has a good selection of spices online, including Bengali five spice and Sichuan peppercorns. It offers free shipping in Australia.

www.aussiespices.com

Vel Spices

Set up over a decade ago, Vel Spices has a physical store in the southeast suburbs of Melbourne as well as a really good online shop. Here you can buy Kashmiri chilli powder, dried kokum and kudampuli, curry leaves and more.

www.velspices.com.au
20 Boundary Road, Carrum Downs, Melbourne

Acknowledgements

I love every part of creating a cookbook. From the conception and pitch to researching and testing the recipes; gathering props, cooking and styling for the photoshoot; editing and fine tuning; before the actual 'birth' of the book and helping it get recognition in the world with marketing and PR. It all takes a lot of time and commitment and there are a number of people who have played their part in its creation who I would like to thank.

Firstly, I would like to thank my parents for accompanying me to India to research the idea for this book back in February 2024; it was hugely memorable and great fun having you alongside me. To my eldest daughter, Allegra, for helping me during my final week of the photoshoot. Thank you for cooking and helping with the styling for some of the recipes. Thank you to my husband Indy, for doing the first editing before it was sent to my publishers – super helpful and supportive as ever. Thanks also to my youngest daughter Zinnia for bearing with me during the many months of endless recipe testing and for your constructive feedback. I know which chapters you loved the most (Indo-Chinese and Tibetan Nepalese for those asking)!

Thank you to the team at Meze Publishing; it was great to work with you all again. To Emma Toogood, for your upbeat positivity, professionalism and can-do attitude – you are always a joy to work with. To Katie Fisher for your patience, calmness and excellent editing; I always feel in good hands working with you. To Phil Turner, for being genuinely interested in the theme of this book, getting behind it and supporting me to write it. To creative director Paul Cocker for running with my rangoli idea for the cover and bringing it to life and making the layout of the book both appealing and user friendly. Thank you also to Maria Alliaud (@mariettis_illustrations) who illustrated the beautiful map of India that appears in this book.

To photographer Tim Green (@timgreenphoto) who did all the stunning food photography in the book. It was so fun to work alongside you again, styling all the shots together in a calm, efficient and professional way.

The reportage shots of India are a combination of mine, the very lovely and talented photographer Holly Peters (@awanderingfoodie_) and Australian designer Briony Timmins, who lives in Bangalore (@bundutextiles www.bundutextiles.com). I have been a huge fan of her stunning dresses for many years and spend most of the summer months in them. Her reportage shots of her life in India are so well captured and transportive. Thank you both.

Thank you also to Kristin Perers (@kristinperers) for putting me so at ease for the portrait shots, which captured the essence of who I am so well.

Some of the props for the shoot were very kindly lent to me by Indigo Antiques, the UK's largest collection of Oriental antique furniture and decorative accessories from India, China, Tibet, Japan and Korea. The next time you are in Wiltshire I urge you to visit their expansive showroom, which is absolutely stunning and the perfect place to pick up pieces for your home as well as gifts, including copies of my cookbook! Check them out @indigoantiques and www.indigo-uk.com. Thank you to Marion and the team for letting me choose some wonderful props for the shoot.

Thanks are also extended to Jeanne, the owner of the beautiful ceramics, textiles and carpet shop M3Tiss in Paris (@m.3.t.i.s.s www.m3tiss.com). I immediately loved the colourful, bold and simple designs when I visited the store. Everything is handmade in France and Morocco and the next time you are in Paris (it's an easy 25-minute walk from Gare du Nord) make sure you pay the store a visit. Thank you so much for loaning me some of your bowls, Jeanne.

I am also very appreciative of the team of recipe testers, who were hugely helpful with their constructive feedback: Sophie, Percy, Rowena, Sasha, Tee, Gina, Jo, Sarah, James, Katie and Charlotte. Thank you all so much.

Finally, my thanks go to you, the reader and owner of this book, for supporting me. Thank you for buying my books and writing reviews and, importantly, spreading the word. I really do appreciate it. As I always say, instead of taking a bottle of wine or a box of chocolates to a friend for supper, take a copy of my book or another book you particularly love – a far more original and thoughtful gift, don't you think? Getting your book out to the big wide world takes time, energy and a bit of luck along the way so finally, thank you to all the independent bookshops that have championed me and my books. It means the world to be supported by you all.

About the Author

Torie True is the author of Chilli & Mint: Indian Home Cooking from a British Kitchen which was published in 2021 and subsequently shortlisted for a Gourmand World Cookbook Award. Torie has been mastering the arts of Indian cooking for over 20 years and inspires others to cook with spices in her cookery classes, demonstrations and book tour talks. A member of the Guild of Food Writers and a Great Taste Judge, Torie lives in London with her husband and two daughters.

@chilliandmint
www.chilliandmint.com

Also by Torie True:

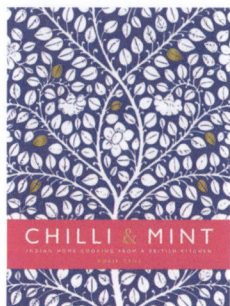

Chilli & Mint:
Indian Home Cooking
from a British Kitchen

Bibliography

An Old Lady-Resident. *The Original Madras Cookery Book* (2nd edition, Madras and Bangalore, Higginbotham & Co, 1881)

Anon. *Dainty Dishes for Indian Tables* (Calcutta, W. Newman & Co, 1881)

Banerjee-Dube, Ishita. 'Modern Mixes: The Hybrid and the Authentic in Indian Cuisine' in *Exploring Indian Modernities* (Springer Nature, 2018)

Burke, W.S. *Every-Day Menus for Indian Housekeepers* (Thacker, Spink & Co, 1909)

Burton, David. *The Raj at Table: A Culinary History of the British in India* (Faber & Faber, 1993)

Carne, Lucy. *Simple Menus and Recipes for Camp, Home and Nursery* (Thacker, Spink & Co, 1919)

Collingham, Lizzie. *Curry: A Tale of Cooks and Conquerors* (Vintage, 2006)

Dalrymple, William. *White Mughals: Love & Betrayal in Eighteenth-Century India* (Harper Perennial, 2004)

Dhondy, Anahita. *The Parsi Kitchen: A Memoir of Food and Family* (HarperCollins India, 2021)

Forster, E.M. *A Passage to India* (Penguin Classics, 1985)

Framji, Navroji. *Indian Cookery 'Local' for Young Housekeepers* (Bombay, 1887)

George, Lathika. *The Kerala Kitchen: Recipes and Recollections from the Syrian Christians of South India* (Expanded edition, Hippocrene Books, 2023)

George, Shalini. *Dakshina: Cuisine from India's South* (Dee Bee Info Publications, 2011)

Gole, Mala. *Hyderabad: A Memory of Taste* (Leiston Press, 2020)

Gordon, Constance Eveline. *The Anglo-Indian Cuisine* (A.J. Combridge & Co, 1904)

Hervey, Henrietta. A. *Anglo Indian Cookery at Home: A Short Treatise for Returned Exiles* (London, Horace Cox, 1895)

Husain, Salma Yusuf. *The Mughal Feast: Recipes from the Kitchen of Emperor Shah Jahan* (Roli Books, 2021)

Jaffrey, Madhur. *Climbing the Mango Trees: A Memoir of a Childhood in India* (Ebury Press, 2006)

King, Niloufer Ichaporia. *My Bombay Kitchen: Traditional and Modern Parsi Home Cooking* (University of California Press, 2007)

Kleeman, Julie and Yeshi Jampa. *Taste Tibet: Family Recipes from the Himalayas* (Murdoch Books, 2022)

Kohlhoff, C.C. *Indian Cookery and Domestic Recipes* (2nd edition, Madras, 1906)

Kottukappally, Thressi John and Salim Pushpanath. *Syrian Christian Favourites. A Personal Collection of Authentic Kerala Syrian Christian Recipes* (Dee Bee Info Publications, 2009)

Manekshaw, Bhicoo J. *Parsi Food and Customs* (Penguin, 1996)

Manfield, Christine. *Tasting India* (Conran, 2011)

Marks, Copeland. *The Varied Kitchens of India: Cuisines of the Anglo-Indians of Calcutta, Bengalis, Jews of Calcutta, Kashmiris, Parsis and Tibetans of Darjeeling* (M Evans & Co, 1986)

Mavalvala, Niloufer. *The World of Parsi Cooking: Food Across Borders* (Niloufer's Kitchen, 2019)

Mavalvala, Niloufer. *The Art of Parsi Cooking: Reviving an Ancient Cuisine* (Austin Macauley Publishers, 2016)

Nair, Sumeet, Meenakshi Meyyappan and Jill Donenfeld. *The Bangala Table: Flavours and Recipes from Chettinad* (Sumeet Nair and Meenakshi Meyyappan Publishers, 2014)

Sahib, Chota. *Camp Recipes for Camp People* (Madras, 1890)

Stewart, Sarah. *The Everlasting Flame: Zoroastrianism in History and Imagination* (I. B. Tauris, 2013)

Sukhadwala, Sejal. *The Philosophy of Curry* (British Library, 2022)

Titley, Norah M. *The Ni'matnāma Manuscript of the Sultans of Mandu: The Sultan's Book of Delights* (Routledge, 2012)

Index

R

raisins

Wedding Pickle 204

Chicken Biryani Mughal Style 216

red kidney beans

Goan Frijoada 118

Nepali Mixed Lentil Stew 150

red split lentils

Mulligatawny 64

Pish Pash 78

Nepali Mixed Lentil Stew 150

Vegetable Dhansak 182

Mori Dar 194

Haleem 210

S

salmon

Fish Curry 116

sausage

Goan Frijoada 118

sea bass

Whole Fish Pollichathu 94

Steamed Fish in Coriander, Mint and Coconut Chutney 190

sea bream

Whole Fish Pollichathu 94

Steamed Fish in Coriander, Mint and Coconut Chutney 190

shaoxing rice wine

Chilli Chicken 18

Savoury Steamed Buns 36

sichuan peppercorns

Sichuan Chilli Sauce 44

Shaptak 158

Colourful Tibetan Steamed Buns 160

Phingsha – Chicken with Glass Noodles 164

Oven-Baked Shaphalay 166

Sikkim Nettle and Spinach Soup 170

Himalayan Hot Sauce 176

spinach

Phingsha – Chicken with Glass Noodles 164

Oven-Baked Shaphalay 166

Sikkim Nettle and Spinach Soup 170

Spiced Greens with Quails' Eggs 214

Hara Bhara Kebabs 222

squash

Fruity Meat Glassy 60

Pumpkin and Tamarind Soup 72

Chicken Stew 96

Pork or Pumpkin Vindaloo 124

Vegetable Dhansak 182

sultanas

Sweetly Spiced Rice Flakes 108

Wedding Pickle 204

swede

Vegetable Dhansak 182

Sweet and Sour Vegetable Stew 200

sweet potato

Sweet and Sour Vegetable Stew 200

sweetcorn

Sweetcorn Soup with Chilli Vinegar 24

T

tamarind

Railway Lamb Curry 52

Frithath Beef Curry 58

Country Captain Vegetables 68

Pumpkin and Tamarind Soup 72

Prawn Peera 104

Fish Curry 116

Chana Ros 120

Chicken Xacuti 126

Goan Pork Sorpotel 128

Pork with Kokum 132

tilapia

Steamed Fish in Coriander, Mint and Coconut Chutney 190

tofu

Savoury Steamed Buns 36

Stuffed Aubergine Cutlets 66

Vegetable Thukpa 152

Oven-Baked Shaphalay 166

Vegetable Momo 174

Keema Samosa 220

tomatoes

Fruity Meat Glassy 60

Stuffed Aubergine Cutlets 66

Allegra's Kachumber Salad 76

Black Chickpea Curry 86

Prawn Fry 92

Whole Fish Pollichathu 94

Duck Roast 100

Arroz Pulao 114

Fish Curry 116

Goan Frijoada 118

Chana Ros 120

Chicken Xacuti 126

Temperature Conversion Table

Centigrade	Centigrade Fan	Fahrenheit	Gas Mark
140°C	120°C Fan	275°F	Gas Mark 1
150°C	130°C Fan	300°F	Gas Mark 2
170°C	150°C Fan	340°F	Gas Mark 3½
180°C	160°C Fan	350°F	Gas Mark 4
190°C	170°C Fan	375°F	Gas Mark 5
200°C	180°C Fan	400°F	Gas Mark 6
220°C	200°C Fan	425°F	Gas Mark 7

©2025 Torie True and
Meze Publishing Limited
ISBN: 978-1-915538-44-4
Written by: Torie True
Edited by: Katie Fisher
Photography by: Tim Green
(@timgreenphoto)
Location photography:
Torie True, Holly Peters
(@awanderingfoodie_),
Briony Timmins
(@bundutextiles -
www.bundutextiles.com)
Styling: Torie True, Tim Green
Designed by: Paul Cocker
Sales and PR: Emma Toogood

@chilliandmint
www.chilliandmint.com

me ze
PUBLISHING

Published by
Meze Publishing Limited
Unit 1b, 2 Kelham Square
Kelham Riverside
Sheffield S3 8SD
Web:
www.mezepublishing.co.uk
Telephone: 0114 275 7709
Email:
info@mezepublishing.co.uk